PLAY
TH
SCOT'
CARD

●

*The Franco-Jacobite
Invasion of
1708*

# PLAYING THE SCOTTISH CARD

●

*The Franco-Jacobite
Invasion of
1708*

John S. Gibson

EDINBURGH UNIVERSITY PRESS

© John S. Gibson 1988
Edinburgh University Press
22 George Square, Edinburgh

Set in Linotron Garamond
by Wilmaset, Birkenhead, Wirral, and
printed in Great Britain by
Redwood Burn Limited
Trowbridge, Wilts

*British Library Cataloguing in Publication Data*
Gibson, John S.
  Playing the Scottish card: the Franco-
  Jacobite invasion of 1708.
  1. Scotland. Invasion, by French military
  forces, 1708
  I. Title
  941.106'9
  ISBN 0 85224 567 X

# Contents

# Preface

*'History is not merely what happened: it is what happened in the
context of what might have happened.'*
Hugh Trevor-Roper (Lord Dacre)

Some twenty years ago when I was researching the naval side of the
'Forty-five, I had the good fortune to be guided by the late
Commander Owen, R.N. (Retd.) who was, and remains, a leading
authority on the Royal Navy in the eighteenth century.

Commander Owen used to emphasise that the supreme moment of
danger from invasion was neither in the winter of 1745 nor in the days
of Napoleon but in March 1708 when a well-prepared invasion fleet
dropped anchor at the mouth of the Firth of Forth. Commander
Owen had written of the naval aspect of this episode in his *War at Sea
under Queen Anne*. Someone, he said, should examine more closely
the accompanying Jacobite conspiracy ashore. From Voltaire to
Trevelyan historians had written off this invasion of 1708 as a feeble
attempt, politically as well as militarily. Commander Owen wondered if they were right.

Over the years, in following the Commander's advice, I found my
way to *The Correspondence of Nathaniel Hooke* as printed, untrans-
lated, by the Roxburghe Club a hundred years ago from over seven
hundred folio pages which had long been deposited in the Bodleian
Library in Oxford. This correspondence of the architect of the 1708
attempt on Scotland was dauntingly vast but of enthralling interest in
showing how it came about, and how it came so close to shattering the
peaceful but still infant Union of Scotland and England. There was
also in this correspondence a hitherto missing part of the inside story
of how the Union was achieved; and no one, it seemed had made
anything but a superficial use of it all. The immediate cover-up by the
disappointed French, the embarrassed English who had been caught
on the hop and terrified Jacobites as they scurried for shelter had
indeed been too readily accepted.

Supplementing the Hooke correspondence are the passionate
history of the Union by Lockhart of Carnwath who was one of the
conspirators; the memoirs and secret correspondence of the government spies (including Daniel Defoe); and the recently catalogued
Hamilton Papers. There are also the famous Memoirs of the Duc de
Saint-Simon and the Journal of the Marquis de Dangeau with their

intimate picture of the court of Louis XIV. Saint-Simon followed the fashioning and failure of the attempt on Scotland with the keenest interest, and his testimony puts it in its wider European context.

In conclusion, I must concede that the central mystery of the conduct of the attempt on Scotland is deepened, not resolved, by what has now come to light. His pilot's journal does not tell us why Forbin failed to shape a course straight for the Forth. The hitherto accepted view, first advanced in the Preface to Defoe's *The History of the Union* and endorsed by Commander Owen, that Forbin kept to the middle of the North Sea to avoid detection, with calamitous consequences for his landfall, has, it seems, now to be discarded. Saint-Simon's verdict has to be our own: suspicions are 'mighty indeed'!

The story begins with the Battle of Killiecrankie in the summer of 1689, as described in the memoir of the defeated commander of the government forces, Major-General Hugh Mackay of Scourie.

In this, and throughout, I have used my attributed sources very closely, rendering written memoirs as narration, speculation, 'stream of consciousness', indirect speech or, occasionally, direct speech. The Notes and Sources section attempts to indicate this without interruption of the main text.

I have many to thank for discussion and advice, including Professor Gordon Donaldson, Dr Bruce Lenman, Dr Rosalind Marshall, Dr Athol Murray, Archie Turnbull and Dr Alice Wemyss. I would, however, wish to take responsibility for the conclusions I have come to over people and events. I owe a large debt of gratitude to the staffs of the National Library of Scotland; of the Scottish Library (Edinburgh Public Library), Miss Meg Burgess in particular; of the Scottish Record Office; of the Scottish National Portrait Gallery and of the Royal Commission on Ancient Monuments and Historic Buildings in Scotland. I have to thank the Bodleian Library for enabling me to consult the original of the Hooke Papers; the National Maritime Museum for directing me to unpublished Byng correspondence; and the historical archivist at the Ministère des Affaires Etrangères in Paris for unearthing the journal of Forbin's pilot. Other debts of gratitude are mentioned in the Notes.

Throughout, Lord Cameron, himself a 'former naval person', encouraged me to research the French navy's attempt on Scotland. My thanks, too, to my wife for forbearance in recent years towards Colonel Hooke, an invisible but demanding presence in our household.

# List of Plates

> 'Advance, illustrious JAMES THE EIGHT
> Now take possession of your right,
> Old Albion for you declares, for you declares,
> The rebel rogues confounded are with fears,
> Scotland unite 'gainst all, 'gainst all that dare oppose,
> Fight, fight and overcome your King's and Country's foes.

*A song at the time of the invasion 1708 to the tune of 'Britons*
*Strike Home'* – The Lockhart Papers I 501.

# Preamble

## The Braes of Killiecrankie

By the middle of the July afternoon they were safely through the pass. A shot from somewhere among the trees across the swirling river had tumbled a trooper from his saddle, but other hint of the rebel clans there was none. By now four thousand foot and two hundred horse had climbed the narrow path by the river's rocky channel, dark with its overhanging trees and the high birch-covered slopes above. Out into the sunlight, red and white, red and yellow, muskets shouldered, long pikes at the trail, came the files of Balfour's and Ramsay's regiments. Then the red-coats of the two new Scottish regiments, Lord Kenmure's and Earl of Leven's, the latter raised in Edinburgh only a few months past. Behind them clattered the cavalry, Lord Belhaven's and the Marquis of Annandale's horse. Lastly Major-General Mackay's own regiment which, with Balfour's, Ramsay's and Lauder's of the renowned Scots Brigade, had served Holland for a hundred years.

*Dutch* troops in the Pass of Killiecrankie? Less than a year had passed since King James, the papist king, had fled to France. His son-in-law the Prince of Orange, the saviour of Holland, the hero of protestant Europe in face of the overweening ambition of Louis xiv's France, had with his wife taken the vacant thrones of England and Scotland. But with French help James was now once more the master of most of Ireland; and in Scotland Jacobite loyalty survived, its strength among the same clans which had fought under Montrose half a century ago. Now, in this summer of 1689, the mercenaries of the Scots Brigade were sorely needed to help the small Scottish army stamp out rebellion.

As the leading companies came out of the pass they were met by Colonel Lauder's advance guard which since break of day had held its northern opening. Before them the high hills opened out to a broad, bare, rising valley, on whose floor glistened great mounds of gravel brought down by the winter spates. In the distance, six miles away, stood Blair Castle, key to the Perthshire highlands; as matters stood, key to all Scotland.

Lauder would have it that the enemy must be further up the valley, somewhere in front of Blair. The general knew better. Lord Dundee, his old comrade in the Dutch service, 'bluidy Clavers' to lowland Whigs, 'Iain Ceann Dhu' – Black John – to the Gaels, had let him through the pass that there might now be a set battle, and this day their long-standing rivalry would be put to the test. But the attack would not come from along the valley. For twenty years Mackay had served the Prince of Orange, and Amsterdam was now his home; his wife a Dutch lady of family. Yet still he was a highlander from Lord Reay's country in the far north-west, and he knew how the clans would fight; that they would come down from the hills, the slope giving speed to their onset. Fifty years ago, Montrose and Alasdair MacColla had first matched highland *élan* against lowland pikes and muskets. Not twelve months past in the braes of Lochaber, Keppoch's men had routed a government force by the shock of just such a downhill charge – and up there with Dundee were Keppoch himself, Clanranald and Glengarry, Stewarts of Appin, MacLeans from Mull, many of Clan Cameron, Frasers from Stratherrick and the Aird. He knew that they would fight with the ferocity of Turks.

A big impressive figure on his white charger, General Mackay halted the regiments in a field of thin corn by the river bank. He ordered forward two grenadier companies and half the horse to reconnoitre, and then, in his impatience, spurred his great beast up the valley that he might see for himself. Armed men held the valley in front of Blair, said the scouts; but the general's gaze was to the steep slopes to the east. High up there, in the distance, as he knew they would be, was the highland host; Dundee's men, a dark swarm in the hills. His experienced eye appraised the intervening distance, and at once he saw the nearness of danger. A highland rabble these wild clans of the west might be, but he knew that from up there Dundee would also have taken note of the wooded knoll half-way down the brae face, and how it might serve as a redoubt from which the clansmen's carabines could pour a harassing fire on the red-coated ranks below. Turning his charger, the general galloped back to the now flattened cornfield by the river bank and hurriedly gave orders for the regiments to follow him up the hillside.

By now the army was complete. Colonel Hastings' regiment of seasoned Englishmen had followed through the pass; so had twelve hundred baggage horses carrying the furniture of war, pick-axes and pike-staffs, powder and ball, bread, cheese, shoes and blankets for the men, sumpter horses with plate and wine for the officers. At the general's command the five regiments turned half-right to follow him up the hill-slope; the formality of European war in the Braes of Atholl, muskets shouldered, pikes glinting in the sunlight, to drive out fear drums beating the slow time of the old Scots march – 'Ding-doon, Tan-tall-on, Ding-doon Tan-tall-on'. They climbed above the knoll of danger to the open ground beyond, where stretched a clearer field of fire over the sloping hillside. There, four thousand muskets crashing in unison would surely put paid to any highland charge. In Montrose's day lowland ploughboys gripping their pikes, half-trained musketeers fumbling with matches, could not withstand a highland onset. Now, in the trained hands of troops in close order, the modern flintlock was surely queen of the battle-field.

The line stretched obliquely up the hillside. Balfour's, Ramsay's and Lauder's were on the lower slope; next, in half battalions six ranks deep, stood Kenmure's and the Earl of Leven's; between them was a wide gap through which the horse could charge to slash at any who had survived the musket volleys. Mackay's, the general's own regiment, was well up the hill slope under their orange colours, the lion flag of the Prince of Orange; and highest of all on the brae face were Hastings' Englishmen. Yet the army's concentration of fire-power could not readily be reconciled with the lie of the land. The clans could so easily keep to the upper hill, come round Hastings' flank, and get between the regiments and the pass. The line must be stretched further up the hillside; and perhaps at this the general felt the first prick of misgiving as he watched six deep become three deep, and the defending hedge of pikes become the thinner.

There they waited as the afternoon ebbed and shadows grew longer. Now the westering sun showed the highlanders much closer, only some three hundred paces up the hill, the babble of their voices clearly heard; and from the drystone walls of a little low farmhouse between the two armies came the first shots of the coming battle as sharp-shooters of the highland army took aim with their long sporting guns. Hoping that this would begin the fight, the general ordered forward a company to clear the hovel; and this they did, but there was no matching response. Then he had the army's four field pieces unloaded from their pack-horses and brought forward to play on the swarming, cheering clans up the hillside; but as they fired each ludicrously broke its leather mountings. The minutes passed, the light began to fade, and anxiety burgeoned. In their past years of campaign against the army of France, in the past three months of march and countermarch through the Grampian wilderness in chase of Viscount Dundee, the Scots Brigade had known nothing like this.

Sensing their unease, the general spoke in his highland voice to the officers and men of his old and trusted regiment. Eight months have passed, he said, since King James fled to France and the Prince of Orange rescued England from a Romish fate. Now the Prince is King of Scotland as of England, but James is in Ireland with an army. It may well be that by now Derry has fallen to him, and with it all Ireland. If Dundee and the clans up there have their way, Scotland likewise will be lost. All over Europe, liberty and the protestant religion will be snuffed out. Above all, he continued, your own safety now depends on how steadfast you are. When the clans charge, fire in disciplined volleys, keep close and firm, and you will see them scamper back to their mountains. They have even stripped off their plaids that they may run the faster when they take to their heels. But if you give way when they come at you, few of you will escape their swords, and any lucky enough to do so will have their heads knocked in by the Atholl folk. So stand like true men!

The general would speak with a confidence he really felt. Few of the Scots nobility were up there with Dundee's rabble. The Duke of Hamilton and the lowland peers were for King William, as were the great men of the north-east. The Earl Marischal had declared for him, and even the papist Gordons were now standing apart. The Marquis of Atholl, for all the Jacobite disaffection of his Perthshire Stewarts, was Williamite too; and surely little was to be feared of the Angus lairds in Dundee's following?

Then, as dusk fell, with a fearful yell and the skirling of their war pipes the highland host began to move. Slowly at first, barefoot, clad in their saffron shirts and tartan doublets, small bonnets scrugged down on their faces, the highlanders came down the hill in a great uneven swarm, their chieftains and standard-bearers on horseback. Two hundred paces away, and they fired their pistols and carabines in a ragged volley, the shot whistling around the red-coated ranks. Some men slumped to the ground. Then the highlanders drew their broadswords, raised targes, and suddenly came on at speed in two dense shouting wedges, one aimed at the general's regiment, the other at Leven's.

A hundred paces away and the flintlocks on the right flank of the Scots army crashed out their volley, as the general signalled Belhaven's and Lord Annandale's horse to break out. Then from the cloud of black smoke billowing in front erupted two great mobs of highlanders; and in seconds, before the line had bayonets plugged into their musket barrels, they were on to it. In horror, General Mackay saw the foot, *his* foot, turn and run as the veteran pikemen, all too thin a hedge, went down to the whirling broadswords. Annandale's horse were wheeling for the charge but seeing the rout, hearing the clansmen screech as they set to the business of butchering, they too faltered, turned about and were off downhill. Belhaven's troopers were no braver, as the highland cascade swept away half of Leven's like so much brushwood. And downhill, away on the left, unbelievably, most shameful of all, Ramsay's and Balfour's, their hundred years of history forgotten, were now breaking ranks and taking to their heels, not a shot fired.

On the hillside, one in four of the clansmen of that terrible onset were dead or hurt to death. The rest were now into the pass, putting fleeing red-coats to the sword in a frenzy of killing. Piled in front of the highland dead were the fallen of the Brigade. Higher up on the hillside Colonel Hastings' men and the half of Leven's which had survived still stood firm. For them as for General Mackay there was nothing more to be done. They could not stop the slaughter in the pass. Their only course now was to get away in the gloaming, down to the river and off to friendlier country beyond the hills of the west.

Here had been the hand of God, forcefully applied: this was Mackay's thought on his defeat as he led the remnant of his army through the swirling Garry and over the hills in the dark of that July night. And, *someone*, he reflected, must devise a bayonet which could be fixed to, not plugged into, the musket barrel so that the volley could be delayed to truly murderous effect.

On this Perthshire hillside, disciplined foot regiments, some as renowned as any in Europe, had been scythed away by a highland charge. For a European power at war with England there was a Scottish card of high value to be played.

Killiecrankie marked the beginning of the Jacobite threat which ended only in 1746 with the disastrous charge across Culloden Moor by the right wing of Prince Charles Edward's highland army. But the 'Forty-five was a dying echo. Far and away the most dangerous of all the Jacobite alarms of the century had occurred nearly forty years before Culloden, when ships of Louis XIV's navy were in the Firth of Forth, aboard them an invasion force which with ready support from an embittered Scotland could stifle at birth the unwanted union with England. The attempt so nearly succeeded in this, and in its twin purpose of bringing the great European war to an early end and in France's favour.

Failure, they say, is an orphan. The importance Versailles attached to *l'entreprise d'Ecosse* of 1708 was matched by its determination to play it down when the invasion attempt was seen to have failed. Success – so the adage continues – has many fathers: why then no hymn of triumph at Westminster? Where luck saves the victor from the consequences of his miscalculation, success can carry its own embarrassment. Queen Anne's ministers had been given the fright of their tortuous lives, yet had to pretend that this had not been so. Today it is clear to see that Scotland, Great Britain and indeed all Europe would have had profoundly different fortunes had not chance and miscalculation afflicted the invasion fleet in the Firth of Forth in the March of 1708.

The beginnings in the opening years of the eighteenth century; the promise; and then the heartbreak of 'the enterprise of Scotland' is the theme of this book. It is all there in the papers of the Franco-Irishman who was its architect-in-chief.

# Part I

## THE
## CONSPIRATORS

# I

# Nathaniel Hooke

To the great men of the Scots Privy Council, their general's disaster was soon no more than 'the ruffle at Killiecrankie'. With the six hundred from Glengarry, Lochaber, the Rough Bounds and the Islands who had gone down to the single volley from Mackay's red-coats there had fallen Dundee himself, his handsome face shattered. Lacking his leadership, the highland army made no headway into the Lowlands, and in 1690 it was soundly beaten on the Haughs of Cromdale in Strathspey. 'The surprise at Cromdell', Jacobite apologists called it, but it was the end of this highland war. In Edinburgh, noblemen and gentry firm for King William stood at the head of affairs; a new bench of judges had been installed; and Stirling Castle, the stronghold of Blackness on the Forth, and the stinking Tolbooth of Edinburgh were packed with Jacobites. To uncover sedition, the crushing of feet and fingers was once more an occasional necessity.

Deposed bishops of the Church of Scotland, and the episcopalian-minded nobility and gentry of the north-east remained staunch for King James' indefeasible hereditary right to the Scottish Crown, however much English prelates and magnates had subverted their own consciences. But they did not translate their obstinacy into action; and sensible men everywhere looked favourably on William, the champion of protestant Europe, himself by birth half Stewart, consort by marriage to King James' elder daughter. In the highlands, only Lochiel, the chieftains of Clan Donald, the remnants of the MacLeans of Mull, and small fry like the clansmen in Glencoe continued under arms; and that was as much on account of their long-standing hatred of 'King Campbell', the House of Argyll. On the east coast, the tiny garrison on the Bass Rock, under its clouds of raucous sea-fowl, alone held out for James; the single frigate of the Scots navy on this coast unable to impede its victualling from Dunkirk.

In Ireland, too, the threat receded with King William's victory on the Boyne. French reinforcements sailed into Kinsale with impunity, the navy of England being in these days unable to blockade Brest; but all was in vain. Limerick surrendered, the city and its walls battered by Dutch artillery; and in the following year the hopes of a landing in force on the English coast were snuffed out with the stiff naval battle off Barfleur and the burning of France's great ships under the cliffs at La Hogue on the Normandy coast. King James, old before his time, was more and more given to his devotions; and his son was a mere infant whom protestant England chose to believe had been smuggled into the Queen's bed to feign a royal birth. While William had no family, James' other daughter, Anne, Princess of Denmark stood next in line, and some of her progeny must surely survive. The Jacobite cause seemed dead.

It did not die: and one man, a Dubliner born in 1664 who had been with Dundee in Scotland, played an essential part in bringing this about. An historical novelist wishing to dream up a character who might embody the political tumult of the late seventeenth century could hardly do better than study the *curriculum vitae* of the young Nathaniel Hooke.

Hooke is 'Hougue', the same La Hogue in Normandy which in 1692 acquired unpleasing associations for Jacobites and the French navy. Nathaniel Hooke's family were an offshoot of the Hookes of Hooke Castle in County Waterford who considered themselves to be descended from Florence de la Hougue, a Norman knight who took part in the conquest of Ireland five hundred years before. Nathaniel's grandfather had prospered as a merchant, his house in the narrow streets of Elizabethan Dublin between the Castle and the Liffey. Though the family at Hooke Castle were driven out by Cromwell's troops, the Hookes, like many other Dubliners, had puritan rather than royalist leanings; and Nathaniel's elder brother married the daughter of Lambert, the Parliamentarian general. After the Restoration this son must have conformed well enough, for in time he too prospered, and became an eminent serjeant-at-law and judge. The Hookes played the middle ground.

In 1679, Nathaniel entered Trinity College, Dublin. He quitted it almost at once, making his way to the college at Glasgow with its rural setting near the still-sparkling waters of the Clyde; and at this centre of more rigid protestant thought and teaching he remained for a year. In 1681, seventeen years old and in the same religious track, he was admitted a sizar at Sidney Sussex College, Cambridge. Perhaps he now found his way to the Green Ribbon Club, the centre of the Whig faction in London which hoped to exclude catholic James from succession to the throne of England in favour of Charles' II's bastard son, the Duke of Monmouth. This is more than likely. With the eclipse of Monmouth in 1683 and the strengthening of James' standing as heir apparent, young Hooke abandoned his education and followed the protestant duke to exile in the Low Countries. In June 1685, shortly after Charles' death, he sailed from Amsterdam in the chartered frigate *Helderenburg*, on Monmouth's desperate venture to displace James as the new king of England.

Twenty-one years of age, newly appointed as chaplain to Monmouth, the young Irishman was rowed ashore at Lyme Regis in company with the duke's curious assortment of adventurers and fanatics. He must have felt the heady excitement of the march to Taunton and the heartening groundswell of popular support, and have shared his half-royal master's disillusion as the gentry of the west country kept their wary neutrality; and there was still no news of the expected rising further north. It was at this first falling of the tide that Hooke was sent ahead through the hostile countryside to London on a mission of the utmost secrecy and danger. His orders from Monmouth were to give 'positive orders for our friends to rise, and that with all the speed they could'.

Young Hooke was now in water far and away too deep. His companions on this mission to the capital had the assassination of King James as their purpose, and Hooke would have none of it. Nor could the duke's friends be persuaded to show themselves. Within a fortnight the Western Rising was over, the rebel army destroyed at Sedgemoor, Monmouth the king's prisoner. Somehow Hooke escaped, though government had learned of his mission when Monmouth's close friend, Lord Grey of Warke, saved his own neck with information about his fellow conspirators. By the autumn Hooke was back in Amsterdam, a fugitive specifically exempted from the following spring's general pardon to rebels. In Holland he consorted with the Monmouth supporters, latterday Pilgrim Fathers who were for setting up a puritan republic in the Americas.

In a London newsletter of the summer of 1688 the following appeared:

> 'Nathaniel Hook, the late Duke of Monmouth his chaplain who was concerned in the rebellion, and hath ever since skulked up and down without being able to attain his pardon threw himself lately at His Majesty's feet, desiring His Majesty's pardon, or to be speedily tried and executed since now life itself as well as the sense of his guilt was wearisome to him; whereupon His Majesty thought fit to extend his gracious pardon to him.'

Sinner come to repentance, or devious young Irishman seeing his chance to benefit from James' toleration of dissenters? Hooke, the erstwhile puritan activist, now went all the way. He joined the Church of Rome.

Within six months James fled the country, and 'the Good Old Cause' that Monmouth had espoused seemed to have come into its own. In later years there was said to be a certain protestant *chic* in having taken part in the Western Rising, but Hooke did not turn back to his old allegiance. Early in 1689 he was in the lowlands of Scotland with Viscount Dundee, whither 'bluidy Clavers' had withdrawn with his loyal following from King James' army. In mid-May, while Dundee was leading General Mackay a dance through the Grampians, Hooke was taken prisoner at Chester, then the port for the crossing of the Irish Sea. As he was found to have on him commissions from James, in those months building an army of re-conquest for himself in Ireland, he was promptly committed to the Tower of London on suspicion of high treason.

The next twelve months were no less eventful. Hooke was a state prisoner of some importance. Gilbert Burnet, the brilliant Scotsman who had become Bishop of Salisbury and William's close adviser, was employed by government to worm information out of him, but seems to have failed; and in his sojourn in the Tower that summer Hooke struck up a friendship with a fellow prisoner, the son of the Williamite Duke of Hamilton. This was the Earl of Arran, at odds with his father, and now incarcerated for his hand in Jacobite plotting.

In July 1689 a writ of Habeas Corpus was moved on Hooke's behalf. In October, Killiecrankie three months past and the highland army eclipsed, he was admitted to bail on heavy sureties. The following February he appeared before King's Bench to be discharged. His early release is curious, there being much Jacobite intrigue in the capital that winter; and it is the stranger in that at once he was off to Ireland, there to take service with King James. Yet there is no suspicion that Hooke was playing a double game. He was at the Boyne in July, and was besieged in Limerick the following year. When Limerick surrendered, Hooke was one of the twelve thousand officers and men who quitted Ireland for France, there to put an Irish sword in King Louis' hand.

Later generations of Hookes had little information about what he was up to in the closing years of the seventeenth century. They thought he served with the regiment of Irish cavalry raised in France and known as the Queen's Regiment of Horse (the queen being Mary of Modena, James' beautiful and pious wife). They also believed him to have been involved in the preparations for cross-channel invasion which began so hopefully in 1692 with the French victory over England's navy off Beachy Head. He was still waiting on the Channel coast with the Queen's Regiment of Horse when invasion hopes were dashed by the English navy's great victory at La Hogue. ('*C'est bien la première fois, donc!* the exile James, ever a monster of tactlessness is reported to have said to his French hosts on their navy's earlier success at Bantry Bay: now, 'King James', wrote Saint-Simon, hardly able to credit it, 'who watched the fight from the cliffs of Normandy is accused of cheering for his own people'.) For Hooke there followed service with the French army on the Moselle until the end of the nine years' war and its hollow victories for France.

With peace restored in 1697 and military men everywhere out of work, the Queen's Regiment of Horse was disbanded, and Nathaniel Hooke discharged. There was no place for him on King James' pension list, crowded as it was with Scots, English and Irish with a whole lifetime of loyalty to the now exiled Stuarts. In search of further military employment he made for Sweden, where the French envoy to the Swedish Court was impressed by this Irish would-be soldier of fortune, and had him employed in his country's foreign service. Now he was Louis' man and *colonel reformé* in the *Régiment Allemand de Sparre* in the army of France. In the tortuous years of diplomacy that followed to avert if possible a renewal of European war, Hooke was in French employ at The Hague. He was well acquainted with Stanhope, the English envoy there, on more than nodding terms with Marlborough himself, and busy gathering intelligence of what was afoot in England and Scotland. He now showed the same passionate concern for the interests of France which he had once displayed for the cause of old King James, and before that for the Duke of Monmouth.

In 1702, European war on the grand scale was resumed over the disputed succession to the Spanish throne. Again it was fear of French ambition which was the root, with the Grand Alliance of England (and so, though reluctantly, Scotland), Holland, Austria, and much of Germany ranged against France; and now there were also in play the commercial ambitions of rival mercantile interests in the warring nations over trade to the Spanish Americas. Even so, King William would probably have been unable to involve England in the war had it not been for Louis' impulsively chivalrous recognition of James' young son as the next King of England while the old exile lay dying at the palace of St Germain-en-Laye outside Paris which Louis had generously given to the Jacobite Court. The war of the Spanish Succession would now also be the war of the English Succession. If recognised as legitimate son to his father, young James would take precedence in his claim to the throne over William's designated successor, his sister-in-law Anne. The war would therefore have a religious dimension, for the court at St Germain was rigidly catholic while Anne was the protestant princess, champion of the Church of England. The conflict with France was confirmed when, soon after the war began, King William died and Anne succeeded.

Hooke died in 1738, *maréchal de camp* in the army of France; behind him a distinguished career in her foreign service; honoured by the king in his appointment to the Order of the Holy Ghost; Baron de Hooke in the Jacobite peerage. In his later years, with the help of his literary nephew and namesake, he arranged his comprehensive collection of papers about the high tide of his long career, the attempted invasion of Scotland in 1708 in the midst of the war of the Spanish Succession. Some months after the old Irishman's death, while his only son, a lieutenant-colonel in the French army, was taking soundings about the sale of his father's papers to pay creditors, officials from the court arrived at his quarters in Toulon to impound them. Thirty years or more was not far enough into the past for the aged Marquis de Torcy who had been Louis xiv's Foreign Minister and Hooke's *patron* and friend in the planning of the Scottish adventure.

It seems that the officials scamped their work; or perhaps their orders were to impound only papers for the year 1708. In the trunk which held the papers, two packages of folio in the small neat hand of Hooke's nephew, marginal comment by the older Nathaniel, did not attract their attention. They have the power to transport the reader back in time to Versailles and the court of Louis xiv in the opening years of the eighteenth century. The Memoirs of Saint-Simon have made posterity familiar with the image of that splendid court at play: how in the evening the entire court would meet in the long suite of rooms that ran from the Hall of Mirrors for music, card games, billiards and refreshments; every room a dazzle of candlelight from chandeliers of silver shining on Savonnerie carpet and motif of laurel, lyre, sunflower and radiant crown. But, Saint-Simon tells us, the king was not there. He was in Madame de Maintenon's apartments, sitting by the fire with her, the wife on whom he depended but did not publicly acknowledge. With them were Colbert de Torcy, Louis' Foreign Minister and Michel Chamillart, his Minister of Finance and War; Torcy, supremely able, Chamillart diligent but grossly over-worked, the king's crony at the billiard table; and as the wits would have it *'un héros au billard, un zéro dans le ministère'*. Then, each morning while the court concerned itself with tittle-tattle and precedence, there would be a council where Louis met his ministers more formally round the great table of green velvet edged with gold, and the serious business of government was conducted. It is this purposeful face of Versailles that the Hooke Papers illuminate.

On a February morning of 1703, the Council had before it a long memorandum from Colonel Hooke on strategy for the conduct of the war. The freedom of its style strongly suggests that it was not the first from this pen for that audience. In his succinct and capable way Torcy would read it aloud *en précis*, as was his custom with papers and despatches. So we too may read it in abridgement. Hooke began with a global view of the war, now in its second year, and he drew attention to the underlying purpose of the English. This, he said, was to damage still further France's financial strength and her trade. He quoted from a paper (how had he come by it?) presented to the English Privy

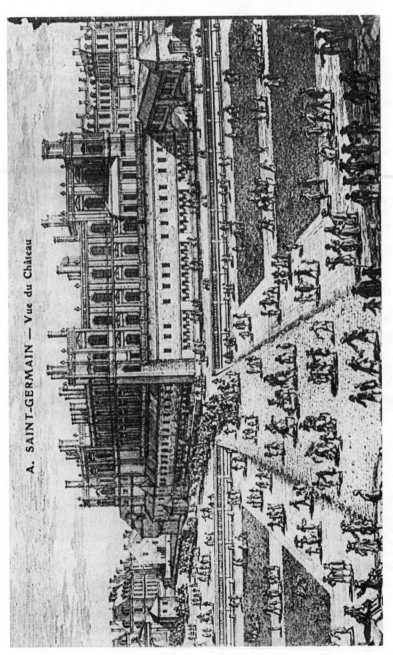

A. SAINT-GERMAIN — Vue du Château

View of the Château of St Germain-en-Laye 'upon a promontory made by a sweeping bend of the Seine'. BBC Hulton Picture Library.

Council before the outbreak of hostilities in 1702. This had made the cold calculation that while England could stand another bout of war, France could not. It presented to English ministers the argument that the time had come through renewed war with France to push for the prize: exclusive trading rights in slaves. The treaty which bound together the Grand Alliance stipulated that England should keep any Spanish territory in the New World that she could seize. To strengthen their hold on trade the English might also be expected to set up a colony in Central America, perhaps in Darien where the Scots had so recently come to grief; and also to strike at France's colony at the mouth of the Mississippi.

France was thus beset by grasping enemies; globally the prospect was ominous. But she had cards in her hand. England and the United Provinces were uneasy partners. The English aspired to supplant the Dutch as world-wide carriers ('*voituriers du monde*'). They were jealous of the Dutch hold on trade to the Orient, particularly the lucrative trade in spices; and they looked with anger on the Dutch herring fleets fishing right up to the mouth of the Humber. In short, the Grand Alliance was vulnerable, and now was the time to break it up before the English Whigs could strengthen their position at Westminster as the party for protestant, Hanoverian succession to the English throne to follow Anne, now Queen of England (and Scotland, and Ireland), but a Queen without a surviving child. The prospect of Hanoverian succession was the cement of the alliance, and the dearest hope of the Dutch. In it they saw the prospect of a protestant England permanently on their side, at odds with France; and they would spend almost unlimited money to bring it about.

But Hanoverian succession was not inevitable; and here Hooke reported on the convoluted state of English politics. The Tories, he said, were firmly opposed to having a German prince for their future king; at the same time, as the party of the established protestant Church of England, they feared the prospect of a catholic successor in the person of the young Stuart prince at St Germain. Nor were the Whigs united; and Lord Somers, perhaps the most intelligent of the Whig magnates, had told Hooke of his personal preference for a Stuart rather than a Hanoverian succession. But the succession was not really the dominant issue in English politics: for the Tories it was to get the better of France, for the Whigs it was to advance their own interests by whatever means lay to hand.

It was therefore the English Tories that France had most to fear; and with them (in over-simplification of the Westminster scene) Hooke numbered Queen Anne's Ministers, the Earls of Marlborough, Godolphin and Rochester. Marlborough, so seemingly open in his manner, in reality so given to dissimulation; Godolphin, the splitter of hairs ('*My Lord Godolphin rafine toujours*'). For all that, if they could get Marlborough on his own during the next summer's campaign, emissaries from France should be able to deflect him both from continued war and a Hanoverian succession; he must surely calculate that his best means of dishing the Whigs and building himself the fortune he so greedily coveted lay in his being the one to arrange the succession of young James to the English throne. It followed that negotiations for peace and a Jacobite succession should be opened secretly with Marlborough in the coming months. These could at least do no harm, and if all they did was to make the Dutch suspicious then they would have served France well.

The horizon toured and the despicable confusion of English politics analysed, Hooke now came to his point. There was a sure way for France to force English ministers to the conference table before this costly European war went any further, and that was to bring Scotland into play. The Scots, he said, hated the English for their engineering of the Darien disaster of 1699, and with it Scotland's hopes for a new source of prosperity in the Americas. Likewise they loathed the prospect of a Hanoverian succession. English politicians were beguiling the Scots with talk of a union in which Scottish independence would be bartered for free trade; but, said Hooke, echoing the views of sensible men throughout the British Isles in these early months of 1703, that could never come about. Scottish animosity towards the English could only grow to new heights in the years ahead.

Hooke briefly reported on the views of the Scottish magnates. These, he said, were simple to understand. (The distinguished corps of Scottish historians who have fished this murky beat of history would not agree, but it is significant that Hooke was so dangerously oversimplifying the scene.) The Duke of Queensberry, the Queen's Commissioner, ('*le grand commissaire*'), had no great following in the country. The Duke of Argyll led the Scottish Whigs and the Presbyterians (who were 'a kind of Church Whig'). Lord Lorne, his son, was distributing Hanoverian money among this party to clinch their loyalties. The Duke of Hamilton – he who as Earl of Arran had been Hooke's fellow prisoner in the Tower of London a dozen years before – led the Episcopalians and many others who were opposed both to a Hanoverian succession and to presbyterian rule. All of this party were Jacobite in sentiment, more or less.

France, he suggested, should therefore take two initiatives. She should put gold into the grasping hands of the representatives to the Scots Parliament of the royal burghs ('*les bourgs libres*'); their votes, thus secured, would lock the door against a Hanoverian succession to the Scottish throne. And, since the English would not stand idly by were this to happen, reviving as it would the age-old threat from north of the Tweed, France should forthwith send a military force to Scotland. War between Scotland and England would be France's salvation; but if France did not move now, and if Scotland's Hanoverian paymasters were given the opportunity to disburse still more moneys to buy support in Scotland, the opportunity would be lost – and so would the Jacobite cause.

Louis XIV had a Frenchman's colourful view of the Scots. *L'ancienne alliance* stretched back into history. Two and a half centuries before, in the darkest hours of the French monarchy, on the battlefield of Baugé seven thousand Scots under an Earl of Buchan had cracked the legend of English invincibility which had dazzled the French since Agincourt. The Latin narrative of Montrose's miraculous Scottish campaign of sixty years past, written by his chaplain but surely the voice of the great Marquis himself, had long been in vogue among military men throughout Europe. In still more recent times there had been Killiecrankie to enhance the unique military standing of the Scottish highlanders.

There was also the curious tale of the hundred and fifty Scottish gentlemen who had chosen exile with James. Louis would surely have heard of this from his late royal cousin, the exile of St Germain, and the romance of the tale, as much as calculation, may well have moved him. The story went thus. After the dispersal of the Highland army in the year that followed Killiecrankie, and in terms of their treaty with William's government, many of the gentlemen who had followed Bonnie Dundee had been shipped from the port of Leith to Havre de Grace in the same way as their Irish counterparts had sailed off to France. That they might continue to serve King James though in French pay, they formed themselves into a company of common soldiers, each subsisting on the threepence a day and the pound-and-a-half of bread allowed their lowly rank; and James had been touched to the heart by their loyalty. In the Nine Years War of the 1690s their company served with distinction in Spain, then in Alsace. In particular, in a night attack on a fortified island in the Rhine, wading through the shoulder-high current, arms linked highland fashion, they had succeeded against the odds. But common soldiers had to make shift for themselves as best they could. Poverty and disease as well as wounds and death took their toll. When peace came in 1697 their strength was down to a score; only their fame lived on in the island they had taken, which had come to be known as *L'Ile des Ecossais*. To the legend of Baugé was added that of the Scotsmen's isle.

It would then have been with a warm, kingly appreciation of the warlike virtues of the Scots that Louis listened to Torcy's précis of Hooke's proposal; and it was perhaps heightened by his intense desire to see England, Scotland and Ireland return to the rightful line of Stuarts. To him Anne was no queen but the Princess of Denmark who had played Goneril to James' Lear. The *émigré* royalties to whom Louis had given the yellow-walled *château-fort* of St Germain-en-Laye, and its adjoining palace, it was they who had the Divine Right to the three kingdoms. Louis and his court, now that James was dead, made much of Mary of Modena, rightful queen of England, Scotland and Ireland, beautiful and tragic, but with hope for the future in her handsome fifteen year old son and lively daughter.

In the king's wife, Madame de Maintenon, seemingly busy with her needlework during the evening discussions in her room, there was another advocate for the Stuart cause. Mary of Modena was as pious and catholic as she. Years later Voltaire learned from the aged Torcy that it was Mary's tears and Madame de Maintenon's persuasion which, in the face of all ministerial arguments of prudence, moved Louis to the fatal recognition of young James as King of England in 1702. Now, in the opening months of 1703, it was Mary's friendship with the King of France's wife which pushed forward Hooke's Scottish project. This she did by securing audience with Louis for a Scottish highlander recently arrived at St Germain; Simon Fraser, who claimed to be twelfth Lord Lovat, chief of the highland Frasers. It was he who had suggested the Scottish project to Hooke.

# 2

# Simon Fraser

Four centuries past, the Frasers, anglo-normans descended from knights of Anjou, had added to their lands in the north-east of Scotland the wild tumbling hill country and kindlier valleys to the westward of the castle of Inverness. Aberdeenshire Frasers had become lowland lairds, but those of the Aird and their ancestral hills above Loch Ness were now clanned gentry, holding to highland ways, their stronghold Castle Dounie, where the Beauly river nears the Firth. The highland Frasers were a force to be respected, as strong perhaps as the following of Macintosh to the south and Grant of Grant in Strathspey, though maybe not quite as powerful as Seaforth and the grasping MacKenzies to the north. To their considerable loss they had found themselves on the wrong side at Montrose's great victory at Auldearn; but, in general, it was their tradition to stand for the Stuarts just as their ancestor had fought for the Bruce. A brother of this tall fair-haired young highlander who now claimed to be chief of the clan, had died of wounds at Killiecrankie. On his appearance in 1702 at the Jacobite court there was ready acceptance for Simon Fraser's assertion that highland chiefs and lowland nobility alike were eager that France should now help Scotland break the regal union with England and have young James for king. He claimed to have sounded the chiefs of the Jacobite-minded clans and enlisted both the Earl of Errol and the Earl Marischal, feudal magnates of the north-east. The message for the Queen Mother and her advisers was that Scotland was ready to rise.

At St Germain, Simon Fraser had first sought out his kinsman, Sir John Maclean of Duart. He had been at Killiecrankie where the onset had been led by the heroes of Clan Gillean; and now Sir John was the very model of a polished Scot abroad, and a pensioner of the Jacobite court. Sir John led Fraser to the Duke of Perth, erstwhile prisoner in Stirling Castle for his adherence to James in 1689, catholic like the king he had served, now Chancellor at the exiled court, and still headstrong as ever for Jacobite plotting. Through him, Simon Fraser was enabled to communicate to Queen Mary (and through her to Madame de Maintenon) his enthusiasm for a Scottish adventure. Louis' Foreign Minister at once put Fraser in touch with his adviser on the political scene in Scotland, Colonel Nathaniel Hooke.

In the opening months of 1703, for fear of English spies and courtiers of dubious allegiance at St Germain, let alone the gossiping court of Louis XIV himself, the plan was fashioned in secrecy. In addition to Hooke, the Papal Nuncio was enlisted, his house in Paris being used for the planning. There was to be a landing of five thousand French troops at an Angus port to form an armed camp to which twenty thousand Scots from the nobility and gentry of the north-east and the clans of the north and west might rally. There was to be a simultaneous descent by a smaller force on the west coast to strike at the Government fort at Inverlochy at the southern end of the Great Glen, and this force was to be equipped with scaling ladders constructed for the task by French engineers. With Inverlochy subdued, the western clans would erupt on the Lowlands, there to join the main invasion force for battle with the regiments Marlborough would be forced to bring back from Flanders.

Simon Fraser's audience of Louis was indeed a singular honour; in Fraser's words, 'never before granted to any foreigner let his quality be what it would'. Saint-Simon's memoirs bear this out. Day-in, day-out, Louis worked at affairs of state with his ministers, but he discussed them with no one else: that is, no one other than Madame de Maintenon. Some of what Simon Fraser (who claimed to be Lord Lovat) had to say in later years of his sojourn in France strains the truth but his cherished recollection of his reception by Louis is perhaps more reliable.

There was no person present except the Marquis de Torcy, who stood behind the royal chair. Lord Lovat enlarged upon the antient alliances between France and Scotland, observing that the Scotch, assisted by the French, had frequently beaten the English, and that, if they were now honoured with the protection of the greatest King that had ever filled the throne of France, they would not certainly be less successful than they had been in former instances.

His Most Christian Majesty replied, with a look of much benignity, that himself and the whole French nation had their hearts unfeignedly Scottish; and that, since Lord Lovat had been chosen to represent the whole body of loyal Scots, he desired to be understood as from that moment renewing with him all antient alliances between the two nations. The king promised at all times to assist the Scots with troops, money, and everything that might be necessary to support them against the English. He added, that he was perfectly acquainted with the fidelity of Lord Lovat and his family, and that he might depend at all times upon his favourable remembrance.

The Most Christian King then quitted Lord Lovat with a most gracious and engaging air, extremely natural to this celebrated monarch. When Lord Lovat retired at the opposite door of the closet where the King had left him, the Marquis de Torcy and the

Marquis de Callières appeared ready to receive him, and had the politeness to say that the King had been highly satisfied with him.

The Scottish adventure was now afoot, and no one other than Lovat, a personable highlander with facility in address as great as his apparent ease in speaking French, could have brought it about. Louis, however, was as much concerned with his royal dignity as with Scotland. Two days later Queen Mary received a visit from him, and in the easy, informal style he used with those few to whom he gave his friendship, he said, 'that he did not know whether Lord Lovat was pleased with him, but that he had been extremely pleased with that nobleman'. He also asked that she should never again seek a private audience for any of her people 'since he had at no other time exposed his person in that manner to any foreigner'. Even so, it was all greatly flattering to Simon Fraser who had now taken up quarters in Paris. Only twelve months past he had been skulking on the hills of the Fraser country; to all other than his clansmen, a rapist on the run.

Five years before, Fraser, then just turned twenty (or so he said) and a captain in the small Scots army, had been embroiled in a bitter dispute over the succession to the Lovat title and the chieftaincy of the clanned Frasers. Their chief had died without a son, and the Marquis of Atholl (whose daughter was the late chief's widow) had sought to have the inheritance descend on the widow's nine year old daughter; the heiress would then be brought up under Murray influence and in due course, to suit Murray ambitions, a marriage arranged with the elder son of Lord Saltoun, head of the Aberdeenshire Frasers. The clanned gentry of the highland Frasers would have none of this. To them the legitimate heir was not the young girl but her elderly relative who happened to be Simon Fraser's father.

In support of his father's claim Captain Simon had raised the clan. Lord Saltoun's son and two sons of Atholl were ambushed, kidnapped and put in terror of their lives. Colours flying, drums beating, an armed Fraser posse made for Castle Dounie where Simon Fraser demanded that the late chief's wife should wed him *instanter*. The lady was appalled.

That night, armed guards broke into the lady's chamber and forced away her waiting-maids. The Minister of Abertarff, 'a poor drunken fellow', was mustered to pronounce Simon Fraser and the lady man and wife. Then there was the bedding, as subsequently described in the record of evidence to the High Court of Justiciary in Edinburgh by Amelia Reoch, one of the maids. She witnessed the happenings because a lady of quality, fully attired, was not easy to disrobe.

About two in the morning, two armed men carried the deponent back to my Lady's apartment, whom she found sitting on the floor, her hair dishevelled, her head reclining backwards on the bed, Donald Beatton pulling off my Lady's shoes, and the Captain [Simon Fraser] holding burned feathers and aquavitae to her nose, her Ladyship being in a swoon. They commanded the deponent to take off my Lady's clothes; but she spurned at the deponent with her feet, shewing the greatest reluctance; upon which, Fraser of Kinmonavie held up my Lady in his arms; the Captain pulled down her petticoats, and sought a knife from Hugh Monro to cut off her stays; but, he having none, the Captain ordered Kinmonavie to cut them off with his durk, which was done accordingly. The deponent was put out of the room; and, when she was going over the close [the courtyard] she heard my Lady's cries, although the bagpipes were playing all the time in the room next to her Ladyship's.

Scottish criminology is a chamber of horrors. Even so, this case is unique.

In the morning, continued the waiting-maid, she saw my Lady's head hanging over the bed-stock, her face swoln, and her Ladyship to all appearance out of her judgment; she spoke none, but gave the deponent a broad stare; even some days after, she did not know her own brother, Lord Mungo Murray; and, when Dumballoch's Lady came into the room, and called Lady Lovat 'Madam', she answered, 'call me not Madam, but the most miserable wretch alive'.

The Murrays now used all their great influence to have at Simon Fraser. In the High Court of Justiciary he was convicted *in absentia* of treason, the law being somewhat twisted to adjudge as treason Simon's raising of the Frasers. Detachments from Atholl's private army were billeted on the Fraser lands, and Simon took to the hills.

In the Earl of Argyll the Marquis of Atholl had a powerful enemy. Only thirteen years before, Atholl's highlanders had been licensed to plunder the Campbell lands when the late earl's attempt to raise Scotland against King James had collapsed. The Campbells were traditionally friends to the Frasers, and in the general pushing for preferment and public position the house of Argyll were rivals to the house of Atholl. Nor would Simon Fraser's escapades necessarily alienate Argyll, a man of notoriously vicious habits. By Campbell influence and Simon Fraser's submission in person to King William, for which he journeyed to Holland, the royal prerogative was exercised to quash the conviction of treason; but the conviction for rape could not be set aside. Back in Scotland in 1702, skulking among his kinsmen, Fraser found to his dismay that with William now dead, the Murrays high in favour with Queen Anne, and the Marquisate of Atholl now a Dukedom, the rape charge was to be revived in a private prosecution at the instance of the lady he had forcibly bedded. This time Argyll could not help him; and in the autumn of 1702 Fraser again made his way to Holland, journeyed through the opposing campaign lines in Flanders and arrived at the Jacobite court at St Germain.

The persuasive story he put about there of a Scotland eager to rise for its rightful king was a cover. Simon Fraser was set above all else on winning for himself the chieftaincy of his clan. If it took a war between Scotland and England to bring this about, then so be it.

At St Germain power, such as it was, now resided with the elderly Secretary of State, Charles, second Earl of Middleton.

Seventy years back the first earl, son of a Mearns laird with a long pedigree, had trailed a pike in the ranks of the Scots regiment which had served Louis' father. Returned to Scotland, a general in the Army of the Covenant, he had given distinguished service as it campaigned first against Charles 1, then for him. Ennobled by Charles 1, he had been a force in Restoration Scotland until he was ousted. His son, succeeding to the title, had served James 11 loyally and well in the brief years of his reign at the Palace of Whitehall; and four years after James' abdication in 1688 he joined him at St Germain. The second earl was a thoughtful man who believed in divinely ordained heredi- tary monarchy – as in their way had Dutch William, Queen Anne and the majority of Britons (even while they explained away the 'birth' of King James' son in 1688 as the smuggling into the royal bed of a baby in a warming-pan). But the religious fanaticism of his late royal master did not touch him, and in retrospect he stands out as one of the few who gave Jacobitism some meaning. In appearance he was 'of a middle stature with a sanguine complexion'. He was also said to be 'the politest gentleman in Europe'. No doubt a decade at St Germain had taught him to recognise a twister when he saw one; his distrust of Fraser was immediate and profound.

A point of principle underlay the animosity. Middleton was convinced that a second Stuart restoration, like that of King Charles in 1660, must come peaceably. Had Middleton had his way, young James would have been educated in England as a protestant. Now, in the early months of 1703, he saw all too clearly that England would never accept a king hedged by French bayonets, and so he rejected Simon Fraser's scheme as absurd. However, being the politest gentleman in Europe, he merely observed that in the proposal he put forward the young highlander 'had not in some places been as careful as authors of romance to preserve probability'. A Scottish adventure could only destroy the prospect of that restoration to all three crowns,

England and Ireland as well as Scotland, which must surely otherwise come about in the fullness of time. Shrewdly, he saw that war in Scotland might serve the purposes of France well enough, but that it could be fatal to the Jacobite cause.

However, Middleton recognised that for the time being Simon Fraser's manipulation had succeeded, and that Queen Mary and the Duke of Perth had outmanoeuvred him; and it was Middleton's name as Secretary of State which was appended to the colonel's commission given to Fraser in February 1703. His too were the instructions issued to Fraser in May to return to Scotland forthwith, there to harden plans for a rising on the grand scale with French help. The commitment of five thousand French troops, arms for twenty thousand Scots, and the outlay of a hundred thousand crowns, called for a more precise involvement of the Scots nobility. But Middleton, distrusting Simon Fraser, was also playing for time; and perhaps Atholl, as the latter's abiding enemy, keeping both St Germain and the Palace of St James in play 'with both hands' (as it was said) had seen to it that the Jacobite court and Colonel Hooke had learned something of Fraser's true nature. So Hooke required that Fraser be accompanied on his mission to Scotland by a naturalised Frenchman and officer in the army of France, Captain John Moray, brother of the Jacobite Laird of Abercairney in Strathearn.

With the help of his patron Argyll, Simon Fraser and Captain Moray reached the highlands. The Jacobite-minded chiefs had been summoned to a council of war in the castle of the Drummonds, close to the edge of the Perthshire highlands. There was the chief of the Appin Stewarts who also influenced the warlike Stewarts of Strath Tummel and Strath Tay; the aged Sir Ewan Cameron of Lochiel in whom a boyhood devotion to the memory of the great Montrose burned as bright as his hatred of the Campbells; and the chief of the proscribed Macgregors. Meanwhile Moray visited the nobility and gentry of the lowlands who were in the know. It was soon clear that the Scots had as yet insufficient appetite for war. Jacobite sentiment was more widespread than firmness of Jacobite purpose.

The emptiness of Fraser's boast to the King of France was now apparent, and he now lost no time in switching to his alternative plan. If the nobility and chiefs of Scotland would not rise for their exiled king, he could yet turn their quiescent Jacobitism to his own advantage by betraying them to the Duke of Queensberry, the Queen's Commissioner in Scotland. Queensberry (as Hooke had noted in his memorandum to Louis the previous year) was short of friends. He had professed to be a Jacobite at heart but was now maintaining himself in power by doing the bidding of London ministers over the Hanoverian succession. Devious as he was affable, he would not now miss an opportunity to discredit his enemies. This chance Simon Fraser offered him by manipulating the letters he carried from Queen Mary to the Scots nobility; by this he could make it appear to Queensberry that Atholl, keen Williamite though he had been, presbyterian though he now was, had plunged into plotting for a Jacobite rising. If a successful Jacobite adventure now seemed unlikely, and with it the prospect of his winning back lands and title for his services to young James and a grateful Queen Mary, Fraser might through Queensberry win the good graces of Queen Anne's government by representing Atholl as rather more of a double-dealer than was normal in a Scottish nobleman in this troubled decade of uncertain loyalties. But he went further than this: he offered to return to France, there to act as a government spy at the Jacobite court at St Germain. In secrecy, Queensberry informed Queen Anne in London of what he had learned from Fraser about Atholl's 'treachery'.

As he had hoodwinked the Jacobite court and Louis XIV himself, so now Simon Fraser hoodwinked the Duke of Queensberry. Or did he? A more considered view might be that Queensberry may have recognised Fraser for what he was, but could not bring himself to miss the opportunity to discredit his rival, Atholl, to Queen Anne and her ministers. That he may have been as false as Fraser is suggested by the commendation he gave to Fraser's testimony: 'My author', so he wrote to Queen Anne, 'is a man of quality and integrity and I dare assure your Majesty there is neither mistake nor trick on his part.' It was high praise for the Queen's Commissioner to accord to one who, as he well knew, was still a rapist on the run.

From another source, Queen Anne and her ministers were now learning of the threat of a French descent on Scotland and of the plans for a Jacobite rising. In his anxiety to canvass the true state of Scottish feeling, Middleton had sent a third agent across the Channel, Sir John Maclean of Duart, he who had introduced Simon Fraser to the Jacobite court the previous year. Disastrously, Sir John had miscalculated the closing date for the amnesty Queen Anne had granted to all who returned home from the Jacobite court-in-exile, and his wife effectively wrecked his attempted secrecy by presenting him with an heir in the fishing-smack which was taking them across the Channel. Sir John was duly apprehended and conveyed to the Tower of London. There, no doubt fearful for his wife and infant child, but certainly in abandonment of his loyalties, he blabbed, agreeing that he would tell all he knew upon assurance of pardon and of being treated like a gentleman; that is, not to be required to testify in public against any person. These twin betrayals, by Simon Fraser and the baronet of Duart, were to have immense consequences.

Immediately, English ministers were given a reminder of the

Simon, Twelfth Lord Lovat. From a mezzotint engraving by J. Simon after Le Clare. Scottish National Portrait Gallery.

chronic need to solve the Scottish problem. Queen Anne was in poor health, a long life was not to be expected. Despite her eighteen pregnancies she was now childless. The Scottish Parliament had already rejected the prospect of succession by a German prince of whom they knew little, unless there were to be the freer trade with England and her colonies which Westminster was not at all inclined to grant. The Parliament in Edinburgh had in the Act of Security of 1702 also sounded a call to arms to give military backing to their stance, and this had been answered with enthusiasm. The Highlands had kept to their warlike traditions. As to the Lowlands, 'the nation was not only empower'd but ordered to rendey-vous and discipline themselves under their own proper officers, as they themselves should chuse; whereupon they armed immediately and rendeyvoused at every parish church in the Kingdom twice a week, which soon brought the whole nation to such perfection of discipline that they could exercise by beat of drum and perform the other parts as well as the regular troops'.

Whether twice-weekly parades could make soldiers of the Cuddie Headriggs of Lanarkshire or Lothian is uncertain, but, in the south-west, the Cameronians who had stood out for Christ and Covenant against Charles II and his brother were still a force to be reckoned with; nor had the great feudal magnates yet quite lost their martial traditions. However, it was the political dangers nearer home that weighed most heavily with the queen's English ministers: the troubles in Scotland now illuminated by Fraser and MacLean gave the Whig opposition a knobbly stick with which to beat the Government. In England the cause of union with Scotland had now at last found a propellant which might just be strong enough to overcome the selfish obduracy of London and Bristol merchants.

In Scotland, the consequences of the 'Scots Plot', as it came to be known, worked the other way. Atholl, finding himself suspected of being a clandestine Jacobite, was so incensed at Queensberry's machinations that he now became an open one; and the clanned force of six thousand from the duke's Perthshire estates was now to be reckoned on the Jacobite side, where their hearts had always been.

By the end of the year, Simon Fraser was back in France, where he could again become the twelfth Lord Lovat (and so we too may accord him the title). In polite enquiry Queen Mary wrote to him from St Germain that,

'The King [that is, her tall, now fifteen year old son] and I are very impatient to hear from yourself an account of your journey, and of all you have done since you left us, and yet more to thank you for the great zeale you have showd for his service and the dangers you have run to serve him. I do assure you we are more sensible of it than I can express it to you, but the King I hope will live to show it you.'

The welcome did not last. Before January was much older the Papal Nuncio was passing on to Queen Mary a report from London that Queen Anne's Council was endeavouring to get to the bottom of the conspiracy in Scotland and that 'there is a lot of talk about a Scotsman called Fraser who is said to be behind the plot . . . The editor of the printed Gazette known as the "Flying Post" who is an extreme

Scottish presbyterian ['un écossais cameronian'] depicts this Fraser of Beaufort as a most infamous person lacking good name and reputation, and says that he was declared a rebel and sentenced by the Courts for having violated the Dowager Lady Lovat, sister of the Duke of Atholl.'

Ten days on and the London informant again wrote to the Nuncio to tell him that 'some say the plot was nothing other than a put-up thing by the Duke of Queensbury and his faction to damage those of the Scottish party known as the Country Party (*le parti de la patrie*) . . . The main target was the Duke of Atholl, and Captain Fraser of Beaufort who is as unfortunate in his reputation as in his undertakings was used secretly by the Duke of Queensberry to get in touch with some of the highlanders and then go to the French Court or to St Germain.'

This last was the inside story which many Scots then and thereafter came to believe about the plot. The rumours quickly revived in Middleton and the queen all their doubts of Lovat. He, in his Paris lodgings, money running out, quickly found that he was no longer welcome at St Germain. In this tight corner, as if he had nothing to hide, Lovat now wrote a lengthy letter of quintessential Simon Fraser to the Duke of Perth at St Germain.

First there was the protest of injured innocence:

'I cannot but tell you even with tears that I am most certainly informed now by my best friends in France that I am made very black by them to the Court of St Germains. O Heavens, what returns to my constant loyalty . . . All the returns I gett is that I am treated lik a doge, like villain and a traiter.'

Then to the threat beneath the bluster:

'The last year I was calld a villain and ane imposture and the Highlanders thieves and robbers and good for nothing else, but they make themselves appear to be the streanth of the kingdom. If I, who hes such power with them, had told them how the Court of St Germains had maltreated me and abused their reputation, they would fight for the Turk sooner then for a King and Queen that would be advised by those who maltreat them . . . I most humble begge of Her Majestie, for Christ sake and for her son's service, to give a character of me at the Court of France to repaire my reputation. If her Majestie refuses this, I hope she will pardon me to acquaint my best friends and her Majestie faithfull subjects how I am usd.'

Yet it was Lovat, not the sagacious Middleton nor the beautiful, pious Queen at St Germain, who was reading English politics aright.

'Tho I be no prophet I dare boldly affirm that Christ Jesus will come in the clouds before an Inglish people or party call home the King; and it is as clear as the sun to any that knowes the countrey that Scotland is the only kingdom willing and capable to restore him, and establish his Majestie sure and absolut in spite of Ingland.'

Lovat then moved to an 'explanation' of his dealings with Queensberry and his fellow magnates in Scotland:

'My Lord, besides the malice of it, what poor silly nonsense is my accusation. I am accused for my conversation with Queensberry, Leven and Argyle. I am said to have made discoverys to Queensberry to betray the Kings subjects, that perhaps my coming to France was to serve him and his government . . . But I begg the Queen may reflect a little on the matter. My speaking and corresponding with these people was the advice of the King's best friends; quhat I told them was to threaten and turn their hearts to the King, quhich I actually did.'

And so on, and so on. The accusations against him were 'stuff and nonsense'. They were all Atholl's doing, and he concluded with a plea for a fair hearing:

'If she [the Queen] heard or suspected any thing of me, she should have examined me befor her Councell befor she shoud suffer me to be so grossly calumniat, for I rather that she shoud order me to be broke upon the wheell then suffer my reputation to be torn in pieces. . . . I wait her Majesties gracious answer, and begg your Grace humbly pardon for all this freedom.'

There was no response from St Germain, though Lovat's hopes briefly revived in March when Lord John Drummond, younger son of the Duke of Perth, came from Scotland to speak warmly (and misleadingly) of Jacobite enthusiasm. It was not enough.

Lovat's chief concern now was that the aversion Queen Mary had come to feel against a Scottish adventure should not be communicated to Louis at Versailles. Towards the end of March it came as a shock to him to learn that Louis' wife had spent two hours with the queen at St Germain. In desperation, he wrote to Hooke of the need to influence Madame de Maintenon in favour of the project. 'This is the tyme to make use of all friends to gain Madam de M for I find the stress of the affair will depend on that at the bottom, which makes me have but melancholy thoughts of it, considering that your Queen's tears are ready and powerfull with the other lady.' His own plight too was worsening daily. 'It's hard that I should starve and ruin by the malice that some have at me, only for my zeal for a French and Scottish interest.'

Eyes were now on Flanders, not Scotland; and for the time being, the Scottish project was frozen. As soldiers moved from winter quarters, ministers at Versailles had the heady feeling that the end of the war was in sight. Thirty thousand of Louis' great army were pouring into the country beyond the Danube. On one side Vienna was threatened by French and Bavarians; on the other by Hungarians fighting for their liberty, helped by French and Turkish money.

The projected invasion of Scotland now temporarily in eclipse, Hooke had to rejoin the *Régiment Allemand de Sparre* in Marshal Villeroi's army in Flanders. Before he left he made one more attempt to keep Scotland on the map, when in mid-May he went to St Germain to take his leave of Queen Mary and Middleton. 'Her Majesty spoke to me about Scotland and sought my views', he reported to Torcy. 'As you told me to do, I spoke my mind, but her only answer was that she was assured that the Scots did not wish to take up arms.' The Queen did, however, ask him to keep in touch with Middleton, in case in his service in Flanders he, Hooke, had an opportunity to communicate with the English [that is, Marlborough].

'The same day', Hooke's report continued, 'Lord Middleton asked me to see him in his study. He talked of Scotland and began by going over all his objections. I answered him point by point until he had to concede that a rising in Scotland would . . . inevitably force the Allies to abandon Portugal and so lead to a peace treaty, and this is what he fears most of all.' Middleton feared the ending of the war as much as he feared its intensification.

Middleton then made a disparaging reference to Lovat, and engaged in some desultory conversation with Hooke which the latter, with his Boswellian ability, duly noted down. Here are the two, fencing with each other.

HOOKE: I must make it plain that I do not believe all that is said against him [ie, Lovat]. I have a high opinion of his zeal. But that is not the central issue.

MIDDLETON: [perhaps in sarcasm?] If it were possible to persuade Marlborough and Godolphin to turn a blind eye to a descent on Scotland and keep their navy out of its way, the enterprise would be made much easier.

HOOKE: I agree that would help greatly but there is little chance of persuading them to do so.

MIDDLETON: You are so taken up with Lord Lovat and his friends that you think well only of their ideas.

HOOKE: I don't know what exactly you are referring to but I

remain firmly of the view that Scotland is ready to rise and that this would be invaluable.

MIDDLETON: I do not disagree. But we do not know how to go about it because of the great distrust the Scottish nobility have for each other.

HOOKE: And so you must begin somewhere, and that means the highlanders.

MIDDLETON: These highlanders just won't trust us! They look only to the French Court. What could *we* do with them?

'As he had now touched on this', said Hooke, 'I pressed him saying that his sense of honour, the Queen's too, and the common interest of both Kings demanded that the highlanders have their way and that he should trust the King of France and his ministers. He made answer that these ministers are so busy that they leave the matter to their subordinates.'

Being the politest man in Europe, on saying this Middleton showed embarrassment (for the subordinate at Versailles to whom Scottish affairs were left was Hooke himself). 'So I did not press him further', said Hooke, 'and he went on to ask me to write to him with a cipher. I did not say no, but I made the poor state of my health an excuse for not being able to do anything at present. So he spoke no more about it.'

Middleton again spoke of Lovat.

MIDDLETON: He is the enemy of the Marquis of Atholl and one must not overlook Atholl's military strength.

HOOKE: [airing the knowledge he had picked up from Lovat] But, my Lord, Atholl is not so powerful as he claims to be. The Stewarts ('*la tribu des Stuarts*') no longer follow him but look more to the chief of Appin.

Middleton, said Hooke, now fell silent, and the discussion came to an end. Hooke, determined as ever, ended his report to Torcy with a vigorous summation of the case for early action in Scotland while, he said, the English Tories were ready to align themselves with the Scottish Episcopalians in the Jacobite interest.

In the months of 1704 that followed, the second colonel of the *Régiment Allemand de Sparre* had much more to concern him than missed opportunities in Scotland. In puzzlement, then in disbelief, the armies of Villeroi and Tallard heard of the march of Marlborough's forty thousand deep into Germany to attempt the impossible, the rescue of the Austrians from attack by the combined and seemingly irresistible forces of France and Bavaria. Meanwhile, in camp with Villeroi's army in Alsace, Hooke learned by letter from the Duke of

Perth that Lovat's duplicity was now plain. It was clear to the duke and to the court at St Germain that Lovat had planned 'by Duke Queensberry's means to ruin the Marquis of Atholl, and to obtain a pardon from Princess Denmark [Queen Anne] for himself and a subsistence. To effectuate the first and gain credit to what he had said, he counterfeited a letter from the Queen to the Marquis Atholl. I believe by this time he is in the Bastille . . .'

However, the Duke of Perth went on fatuously to assert that there was enough in the information coming across the water 'to convince the Queen, the King of France and everybody of the determination of many in Scotland to venture all for the common interest'. Hooke received the duke's letter in the first days of August 1704, and on the 5th he reported its contents to Versailles. Within a week Tallard's army was destroyed at Blenheim and the war's course changed utterly.

Lovat was not sent to the Bastille. Hooke's pleading that he was not as black as had been painted may have had its effect; but for the moment he was consigned to detention in the Château d'Angoulême, deep in provincial France. His large physical presence moved out of the Jacobite story, not to reappear until the rebellion of 1715 set Scotland ablaze. (In that episode, by an adroit change of sides, he was able to win back lands and title in securing his clan and much of northern Scotland for King George.) In the meantime he was to remain the significant influence throughout the planning and execution of the attempt on Scotland which would now be made, for his had been the inspiration behind *l'entreprise d'Ecosse*. In that he had mortally offended the King of France by making him his dupe, Lovat's malign influence would be its downfall.

When Lovat first came under a cloud of suspicion at St Germain and Versailles in the spring of 1704 after his return from Scotland, he had compiled for Hooke a lengthy memorandum on the justice of his claim to the Lovat peerage. This seems to bear out what legal opinion today endorses, that Simon Fraser's claim to be the twelfth Lord Lovat was well-founded in Scots law and that the then Marquis of Atholl had indeed been guilty of sharp practice in seeking to have the succession dwell with his daughter, the dowager. It also brings out the contempt highland pride felt for the grasping Murrays. Forty years past, the Marquis of Atholl 'had not a hundred pounds a year . . . but was forced to live in a turf house at Tillimelte and depend only upon what his company of banditti forced from his vassals the Stewarts of Atholl who to this hour would cut his throat'. Thus it was, said Lovat, that the marquis designed to have for his sons 'who had not a groat of their own' the fertile Lovat lands round Beauly. Simon Fraser had therefore seized Atholl's sons to prevent the loss of his proper inheritance.

This much is believable, but it leaves the enforced marriage to be explained away. Lovat's voice coming to us across the centuries is almost equal to the occasion:

His [Lovat's] kindred and relations, finding that he had committed a great riot in seizing those Lords, and riseing his men against the laws with displayed colours, were afraid that my Lord Atholl, by the power his son had in the Government, would get all the laws and forces against them. They advised him to marry the widow, who professed to every body that she loed [loved] him, and who sent him invitations by her doer [steward] in the country. All his friends concluded that this would make a peace with Atholl, . . . The Master of Lovat being but then 20 years of age, he had no inclination to marry, especially a woman that might have been his mother; however, his relations assuring him that marrying of her was the way to keep out my Lord Atholl, or any other, from having any footing in the countrey, which they might have by her annuity, he was at last perswaded to that fatal marriage, which was the cause of all the disasters his fortune, reputation, and kindred sufferd ever since. The lady was overjoyd at this resolution, and marry'd him with all the apparent desire in the world, and liv'd with him near two months more cheerfully and affectionately than ever she was seen to do with his cousin her former husband.

Note that Lovat pleads his youth as additional excuse for the affair of the Dowager; this no doubt on the grounds that much may be forgiven at twenty which is inexcusable at thirty. Lovat is caught out by this falsehood. College records do not usually lie, and it is clear from the register of King's College at Aberdeen that Simon Fraser, who matriculated there in 1684, was thirty – not twenty – when he took his cousin's widow by force. A man who so to exculpate himself would lie about his age would probably lie about anything.

# 3

# James, 4th Duke of Hamilton

'They have just brought us tidings so strange and disastrous that I am afraid my servants have misunderstood them,' Madame, as Louis' sister-in-law was known, wrote one day in the August of 1704. 'They say that the enemy have captured twenty-six battalions from Maréchal Tallard, and they are not sure that he himself is not taken prisoner.' A week later Versailles was still in the dark about the disaster to French arms on the Danube. 'We do not know yet exactly what has happened,' wrote Madame; 'It is well known that Tallard has lost the battle, but how he did so is not known, and we do not know the exact extent of our losses.' By the very end of the month news was coming across the enemy lines from husbands, lovers and sons. 'One sees mourners everywhere. It is all lamentable and war is a horrible thing.' The king was puzzled that the hand of God should have chastised him so.

In the autumn Louis and his ministers were quick to regroup their armies as Marlborough, moving into Alsace, sought to position himself for an invasion of France the following summer. In November, Landau fell and Trèves was threatened. By the end of the year France could fear, and the allies look forward to, a campaign the following summer along the valley of the Moselle. Once more in Paris to watch events in Queen Anne's three realms, Hooke took note of the rising tide of anger between Scotland and England; and he thought of the possibilities of military initiative in Scotland to relieve the threat on the Moselle. The report in the *Gazette d'Hollande* of a speech at Westminster by the High Tory peer Lord Haversham about the threat from Scotland had alerted him to the possibilities. Lords and Commons were still making much of the danger of a backdoor invasion of England disclosed by Sir John MacLean and Simon Fraser; and anti-Scottish speeches at Westminster were breeding anglophobic reaction in Edinburgh.

In January, Hooke opened his attack on Louis' ministers with an approach to the Papal Nuncio, and by laying siege to Torcy himself. 'The breach between Scotland and England widens every day,' he assured the latter; and under the Dukes of Gordon and Hamilton the Scots seemed to be united against the English. Hooke also sought an ally in the Maréchal de Villeroi, commander of the army on the Moselle. Since the anger of the Scots against the English was now so intense, said the memorandum he presented to Villeroi, France should send a trusted envoy to Scotland to bring back Scottish delegates with whom Versailles could negotiate. Scotland's military potential made her inflammable material, and the time was favourable for action. In their belief that France would not help Scotland, the English made no pretence of hiding their contempt for the latter. Now that the whole of the English army was in Flanders, the present plight of the Scots was France's opportunity.

At St Germain, the Duke of Perth was next brought into play, but he needed no prompting. While Middleton was all for caution and the waiting game, Perth as ever was predisposed to Scottish adventure. His sister, the recently widowed Countess of Errol, had written to him from her castle of Slains on the Aberdeenshire coast pleading for immediate military action in Scotland to raise the country under the Duke of Hamilton. The Duke's attitude would indeed be crucial. Bonds of intermarriage made something of a unity of the Scottish magnates, and they looked to Hamilton for a lead. Perth assured Hooke that Hamilton was indeed ready to take up arms. His recent absence in England had made people wonder; but Hamilton had let it be known that he had only gone there to draw his rents from his wife's Lancashire estates, being, as ever, chronically short of money. For her part, said Perth, the Countess of Errol had sent emissaries to the Highlands to sound out the clans. Queen Anne had made a foolish appointment in raising the youthful Duke of Argyll to be her commissioner to the Scottish Parliament, now that the Duke of Queensberry and his fellow minister the Marquis of Annandale had lost her trust. 'These two', he had pleasure in noting, 'do all they can to hinder the boy's having better success': a massive underestimate, indeed, of the twenty-seven year old Argyll who had now succeeded his father, Lovat's friend.

A possible Irish dimension to the plan was also emerging. The Irish, Hooke wrote to Torcy, would surely rise if Scotland took up arms. It was clear to him that England was now threatening to put Scotland under her heel just as she had trodden on Ireland. The joint resentment of the two kingdoms could be used to bring England down.

By the end of April 1705 Hooke had secured his first objective: Torcy and his fellow ministers were now again thinking seriously of Scottish possibilities. This attained, the need was to agree how discussions with the Scots should be opened. Could a Frenchman be sent under the guise of a Huguenot refugee, or of someone who had fled the country on account of a duel? For the first time in Hooke's correspondence James Carron (*le sieur Carron*), a Scot, is now mentioned. Carron's seamanship had already been put to good use in secret voyages to Scotland. He knew the outposts of Jacobite loyalty on the east coast: the Countess of Errol's Slains, the Earl of Marischal's great castle of Dunottar on the cliffs of the Kincardine coast, and the Ogilvie castle of Boyne, near Banff. For all his years, Perth now pushed on the planning, seeking out a still reluctant Torcy at Marly – 'that little toad, de Torcy' as Madame called him, a view perhaps shared by the hasty Perth. Louis' ministers were disposed to await the arrival in France of emissaries from the Scottish Jacobites; and the continuing antipathy of Middleton at St Germain to any Scottish adventure no doubt made it the more difficult to bring Torcy to a decision.

In that May of 1705, as Marlborough made the opening moves in the summer campaign along the Moselle, Hooke was loath to rejoin his regiment until a decision was taken about Scotland. But his politicking since January had used up all his funds, and he had not the means to rejoin. Short of money though he was, he did not lack self-confidence; and so he engaged the interest of the king's intimate, the Duc de Chevreuse, who duly wrote to Torcy recommending a 'grati-fication' to enable the colonel to return to the Army of the Moselle.

Towards the end of May, by now somewhat desperate at the want of decision about Scotland, Hooke again wrote to Torcy. It had now been decided that Carron should be given command of a ship to take dispatches from St Germain to the Scottish Jacobites. Surely she should carry an emissary from Versailles to persuade the Jacobites to take up arms in the way the Hungarians had risen against Austria? The Scots more than ever were at loggerheads with the English; witness the recent uproar in Edinburgh 'which forced the Privy Council to have three English officers hanged despite the pardon they had received from the Queen' [the savage, anglophobe killing of Captain Green and the officers of the *Worcester* on a false charge of piracy]. The emissary from France which Carron's frigate should carry would also cut down to a reasonable level such demands for help as the Scots might make.

At St Germain, Perth now wrote to Torcy assuring him that his sister at Slains could make all arrangements for the reception of an agent from France; and Hooke wrote to Chevreuse asking him to use his influence with Torcy 'to speak to the King in my favour'. Within the charmed circle round the king, Chevreuse was, as it were, a minister without portfolio, present at the Council and with a hand in the day to day conduct of the war. (Few were aware of this; at this stage not even Saint-Simon, but Hooke knew his Versailles.) On the last day of May Chevreuse replied. Get the Duke of Perth to work on Torcy, he said, that he may remove the Foreign Minister's continuing objections to a Scottish adventure: and Hooke himself should go to Scotland as the emissary of France, thus removing the difficulties being put in the way of a voyage to Scotland. In grateful acknowledgment, Hooke responded the same day from St Germain. He would speak to Perth at once. Indeed he would have gone to Versailles that day but for the Whitsunday Ceremony of the Order of the Holy Ghost which would take up the whole of the morning. He also confessed to extreme nervousness at being seen around the court when military men should be with the army.

It was now the early June of 1705. Hooke had a successful audience of Queen Mary at St Germain, she saying that she agreed that someone should go to Scotland. 'I watched the Queen's demeanour while she spoke', Hooke wrote to Torcy, 'and as her true feelings shew in her face, I am quite sure that she is for this plan.' The Queen said that she would speak to Louis when she saw him on Sunday. 'I very much wanted to press her to make it sooner', wrote Hooke, 'but I did not dare to do so, believing it better to lose a day or two rather than bring to ruin a matter of such importance . . ..' The queen spoke of the divided counsels at St Germain, and of her suspicion that there was treachery about; but her support for the Scottish adventure was now unhesitating, and she put the question which Hooke surely wished to hear. Would the colonel be prepared to go to Scotland if Louis selected him? 'I said yes, and she replied that she was very happy about that.'

The danger of his falling between two stools gave Hooke anxiety, but his concern on this account was soon over. Within days a note came from the Duke of Perth at St Germain. 'You know, my dear Colonel, how I am situate at the King's table, the King being betwixt the Queen and me. She was so impatient to tell me the news that she whispered to him to tell me that she had spoke, and that what she asked would be done . . . I wish Mrs Hooke and you good rest.'

Queen Mary had used her influence with Louis. The mission to Scotland was approved. Colonel Hooke was to be the envoy.

Four weeks later, seasick, fevered and spitting blood, Hooke lay wretchedly in *L'Audacieuse*, the frigate which Carron commanded for the mission to Scotland. It had not been easy to secure such a good ship of the king's navy, swift through the water, already with a reputation for her commerce-raiding in the North Sea along with the renowned Dunkirk privateers. Yet, on the whole, preparations had gone smoothly. Hooke had compiled and Torcy (and Louis) had approved a lengthy mandate for the mission to Scotland, setting out the arguments to be deployed and the negotiating objectives to be attained. Letters from Louis and from Queen Mary to the Scots nobility had been written. Though a week of summer southerly winds had been lost while Hooke at Dunkirk had awaited the arrival of

Panoramic view of Edinburgh from the *Theatrum Scotiae* by John Slezer, 1693.

money and letters of credit, *L'Audacieuse* had been crewed, provisioned and given privateering instructions to serve as a blind. She had also been given signals to display when lying off Slains so that Carron might learn whether the coast was clear. From St Germain, the Duke of Perth had given Hooke his detailed evaluation of the loyalties and military capabilities of the clans of the highlands and the great feudal families of the lowlands and the north-east. He also gave Hooke a letter for his sister, the Countess of Errol. 'You could not believe', he wrote to her, 'how highly the King of France and his Ministers value and esteem Colonel Hooke.' Lastly, he wrote in kindly terms to Mrs Hooke; her husband's mission was secret but she could be assured he was well. That Irish lady, one of Queen Mary's ladies-in-waiting whom Hooke had married two years before, would be grateful for this indication of the duke's fatherly concern for her: she was now with child.

Ten days out from Dunkirk, *L'Audacieuse* making no headway against the northerly winds, Carron decided to return to Dunkirk roads and disembark his sickly passenger. The mission to Scotland was for the time being frustrated, but it was not in Hooke's nature to give up. By mid-July he had sailed again.

Three months later, as happened every year, Louis' court moved from Versailles to Fontainebleau; to the renaissance charm of that palace and to hunting in the great forests. In that autumn of 1705, newly returned from Scotland, Colonel Hooke came to Fontainebleau to report his adventures; also to answer the question in Torcy's mind – was Jacobite feeling in Scotland at such a pitch as to warrant a military adventure from France which might force Marlborough and his regiments home from Flanders? Within days of his arrival, as he noted in its margin, the report of his dealings with the Scottish magnates came before the King's council.

When he got away from Dunkirk in July, Hooke had been at a low ebb with the sickness that had afflicted him on the abortive attempt to reach Scotland earlier that month; and he felt doubly wretched at having to leave his wife at St Germain without a word about his hazardous mission. But his duty was his physic.

The report he now presented to the King's council began with his departure from Dunkirk.

The second time I went aboard the royal frigate *L'Audacieuse* the wind was so much in our favour that by noon on the fourth day I reached the northern part of the province of Aberdeen and the castle of the Earl of Errol, Hereditary Lord High Constable of Scotland.

This was Slains, the great house which was so to impress a later visitor, Dr Samuel Johnson on his way to the Hebrides: Slains which today stands eerie and roofless on its cliffs above the North Sea.

As soon as M. Carron who commanded the frigate had made the signal he had agreed on his previous voyage, the Countess of Errol, mother of the High Constable and sister of the Duke of Perth, sent out a rowing-boat, and M. Carron disembarked with me. The Earl of Errol was at Parliament in Edinburgh which had been sitting for three weeks; and his mother gave us a warm welcome. She is a lady of about fifty and has a thoughtful and penetrating mind; everyone who is well-affected (*bien intentionné*) trusts her. Knowing her to be fully informed about what was going on, I remained with her for two days to learn how matters stood in Scotland and the views of the most important of the nobility.

When Hooke had handed over the letter he carried from Queen Mary which invited Countess Anne to speak freely to him, his hostess said ominously that he 'would find matters to be a great deal changed'.

Lady Errol had, indeed, disturbing news to impart. The excitement which Lovat's mission aroused among Scottish Jacobites twelve months past had now abated. Despite his great name, the Marquis of Montrose had gone over to the Court party. Since nothing could be done for young King James, as he said to his friends, he would look to his own interests; (he would indeed soon be a duke). Among the nobility mutual distrust was rife; and though from his realm in the north-east the Duke of Gordon had sought to unite them in the Jacobite cause, he had had no success. Worst of all, Hamilton, the premier duke, supposedly leader of the Scottish patriots, had refused to co-operate with Gordon or, indeed, with anyone else. 'All this,' said Hooke, 'gave me great anxiety, but I resolved to go to Edinburgh and see what I could do.'

Meanwhile *L'Audacieuse* rode at anchor close to the castle; and on the second day Hooke felt alarm when a sail coming up from the south was seen to be one of the three frigates which made up all there was of the diminutive Scots navy. However, the countess calmed his fears, sending one of her gentlemen out in a rowing boat to ask Captain Gordon of the *Royal Mary*, to make himself scarce. 'This he did since the lady had won him over; and as he sails up and down the coast he is careful to give her warning of his presence. For his part the captain of *L'Audacieuse* now agreed with M. Gordon how they might keep out of each other's way.'

Hooke now instructed *L'Audacieuse* to sail to Norway, there to wait for three weeks before coming back to Slains, by which time there should be some information about the affairs of Scotland to send back to France. In company with a young gentleman whom the countess had arranged as guide, Hooke set out for Edinburgh. They avoided Aberdeen and the curiosity of other burgh towns on the way, and by dint of three days hard riding reached Edinburgh early one August morning.

The journey from Buchan to the Lothians lay through an unenclosed countryside, and since August had only just begun the rigs of oats and barley would still be unripened. It was a countryside with roads unfit for carriages but with the houses of the gentry, hitherto built for defence, now to the eye of one English visitor at least beginning to be 'modish, both in fabric and in furniture, even though they want their gardens, which are the beauty and pride of our English seats'. As for ordinary folk, they wore bonnet and plaid, and lived in earthen-floored houses of loose stones, roofed with turf. On the way south Hooke and his escort would have to undergo the ordeal of the Scottish inn, where they would be fortunate if they had a room to themselves and their dinner would be none too cleanly served by a barefoot lassie. But there would be a rough plenty of French wine and brandy, served in pewter flagons.

Edinburgh was as yet a city with little thought of pushing her housing beyond the far side of the ravine of the Cowgate or into the fields above the Nor' Loch. A garrison of the small Scots army held the castle. From Lawnmarket to Netherbow port was the one *grande place*, its unity as yet unbroken. Swarms of beggars were everywhere: but there were apple-trees and arbours in the gardens of the quality off the Canongate, and nearby was 'the Abbey', the palace of classical baroque which Charles II had rebuilt. Duly arrived, Hooke sent his escort in search of the Earl of Errol; no doubt the celebrated corps of Edinburgh caddies would quickly put him on the right road. However, Errol, more cautious than his mother, did not come in person; but he sent an emissary, one Charles Fleming, catholic as well as Jacobite, and brother of the Earl of Wigton. Could contact be made with the Duke of Gordon, asked Hooke? In fact the duke had left that morning for his great house in the north, but his duchess was still in town, at her house on the Castlehill. (For several years duke and duchess had led separate lives). That night, mindful that he had met the duchess fifteen years before in the spirited months of 1689 when he had come to Scotland to assist Dundee in raising an army for King James VII, Hooke set out with Fleming as guide, to meet her again.

At last he had found an ally in this English-born lady, herself the daughter of a duke. She had indeed to be deterred from fetching her husband back to town. This would have attracted dangerous attention, for the duke's escort of a hundred followers would have returned with him, but the duchess sent a servant to overtake her husband and his posse of Gordons so that he might have the letters Hooke had brought from the King of France and Queen Mary. She also helped Hooke find a safe retreat 'because', said Hooke, 'hostelries are too public and the city of Edinburgh is so small that you only have to appear twice to be recognised and to become the subject of gossip'. She put Hooke into the care of one Father Carnegy, a catholic priest related to the Earls of Northesk in Angus; at daybreak he had Hooke out of Edinburgh to the old tower-house of Comiston. 'Lady Comiston' (a courtesy title) was the widow of a wealthy Edinburgh lawyer who had bought an estate on the gently-rising wooded ground between the town and the Pentland Hills, and in her old age had turned catholic (but, it seems, kept quiet about it). Comiston Castle was therefore a convenient and secure refuge, the more so since, as Hooke noted, 'she had a secret room in the house to harbour missionaries in times of persecution'. There Hooke was to remain throughout the month of August.

Father Carnegy had another essential role to play in that he was close to the Duke of Hamilton. Hooke would recall the handsome young nobleman who for six months from the summer of 1689 had been his fellow-prisoner in the Tower of London. Prior to that, as Earl of Arran, heir to the Hamilton dukedom and descendant of the two successive Dukes of Hamilton who had given their lives to the royalist cause in the Civil Wars, he had enjoyed the patronage and friendship of both Charles and James. By 1688 he had been a Gentleman of the Bedchamber and had command of a regiment of horse with the rank of Brigadier General. In marked contrast to John Churchill, that other royal favourite, he remained true to James when his royal master fled to France. 'I cannot violate my duty to my master,' he insisted as he confronted the Scottish peers. 'I must distinguish between his Popery and his Person.' Within a year he was implicated in the very first plot to bring about James' restoration, and it was for this that he was consigned to the Tower. At that early stage in his life he appeared a dashing, romantic figure; Hooke looked to him now as the patriot who could unite his country against English domination and Hanoverian succession alike.

In 1695 his choleric father died. Three years later, on his marriage, Arran was given the title of James, 4th Duke of Hamilton while his mother, duchess in her own right, retained Hamilton Palace and the wide Hamilton lands in Lanarkshire and the Lothians; and so her eldest son was constantly short of money. By 1705 he was middle-aged, heavier-jowled, reddish-faced, more imperious than the handsome blade of his youthful portrait. His family took a disenchanted view of him; particularly so his mother. His extravagance was a constant menace to the hard-won solvency of the Hamilton estates; he

James, Fourth Duke of Hamilton [in 1703] by Sir John Medina. In a private Scottish collection.

did not attempt to disguise his preference for London society to landowning in Scotland; his refusal to settle down even after his second marriage (to a shallow and somewhat peevish heiress with great estates in Lancashire who was presenting him with a succession of young Hamiltons) all confirmed the old lady in the disillusion she had for years felt towards her eldest son. Now that he was posing as the leading man in the Parliament in Edinburgh, her dismay was all the greater; settled policies he had none, and it was not possible to fathom his purpose. Perhaps if the level-headed girl who was his first wife had lived, things might have turned out differently; the sincerity of his feelings for her had been the only certain feature of his life.

Neither did his contemporaries know quite what to make of Hamilton. He had put himself forward as leader of all Scots incensed by the Darien disaster, but Jacobite nobility such as Errol who were disposed to look to Hamilton for leadership on account of the great name he bore, were infuriated at his devious ways. They had already seen his intemperate jealousy of the Queen's Commissioner, the Duke of Queensberry, hinder the emergence of the solid majority support that existed in Scotland for the eventual restoration of the royal exiles of St Germain; and this had allowed the presbyterians a strength in Parliament out of all proportion to their limited following in the country. He had also made it clear that he would act contrary to the views of his Jacobite following if he felt so inclined. The year before, he had flouted their wishes in the matter of selecting members of the Estates of Parliament to represent to Queen Anne the true state of feeling in Scotland: Hamilton's selection had been a gift to the Whigs. Yet he had charm to match his pride; and he could readily command devotion from a following just as eager to give it to him, for deference was owed to the premier duke. The passionately Jacobite George Lockhart of Carnwath who was to chronicle the demise of old Scotland conceded that he was 'selfish and revengeful . . . in all his designs'; and yet this Lanarkshire laird could not quite bring himself to believe the worst about the Lanarkshire grandee. Hamilton was to him 'master of an heroick and undaunted courage' who could have 'made as great a figure in the world as any other whatsoever and that either in a civil or military capacity. Never was a man so well qualified to be the head of a party as himself.' 'Since 'tis certain,' Lockhart continued, 'there's no mortal without some imperfection or other, and that his were so small and inconsiderable in respect of his great endowments and qualifications we may well enough pass them over and conclude him a great and extraordinary man . . .' Even young John Clerk of the Penicuik family in Midlothian and a Queensberry protégé, saw Hamilton as courageous as he was affable and eloquent.

Hamilton the patriot duke, the emblem of loyalty to the exiled Stuarts, might have been perceived otherwise had Lockhart and his friends witnessed the secret meetings now taking place in the Palace of Holyroodhouse between the duke and Colonel Hooke.

In preparation for these, Hooke met both the Earl of Errol and his fellow magnate of the north-east, the Earl Marischal. The latter's province was the Mearns, the cold, undulating, and as yet unimproved country south of Aberdeen, which he commanded from his clifftop castle of Dunottar. Like Errol, the Earl Marischal was in Edinburgh for the session of Parliament. Just as at Slains it was the Countess of Errol who was a moving spirit for the cause, so in Edinburgh it was her niece, the Countess Marischal, who helped keep up the Jacobite momentum.

Fleming, as go-between, brought the Countess Marischal to Comiston on the first morning of Hooke's sojourn there. She told Hooke that her husband was anxious to see him and would do so that evening, but that the Earl of Errol was making difficulties and had refused to see Hooke unless the Duke of Hamilton likewise consented to do so. Meanwhile, he wished her to ask Hooke what proposition he had to make. Hooke's response was sharp. The Lord High Constable, he replied, misunderstood how matters lay. As an emissary from the King of France, he, Hooke, had no proposals to advance; on the contrary he had come to listen to what the Scots had to say. It was they who had requested help from France; and it was simply out of respect for the young Stuart king and the old alliance between France and Scotland that Louis had sent him on this mission.

The Countess said she would retail this to Errol. She then asked if Hooke had brought any money with him. 'I saw from this,' Hooke noted, 'that they were worried lest they be put to expense. I said that I had brought with me enough money for what had to be done, and that I was ready to defray any necessary expenditure they might have to incur.' The Countess left, and Fleming was soon back at Comiston with a message that both Errol and the Earl Marischal would see him that evening. Towards nightfall, Hooke rode into Edinburgh to wait on the Earl Marischal.

He found a man of about forty, a persuasive talker, very proud, not to be outdone by anyone in his declared devotion to the king over the water. He had also dined too well. 'If he were not so given to the bottle,' Hooke noted, 'this would be a great man.' They were joined by the Earl of Errol, a younger man, who seemed to Hooke both firm of purpose and knowledgeable and – he also noted – 'without any obvious vices'. Errol was a man of few words, but when he spoke it was to say that he was prepared to stake life and fortune for the Stuarts. 'To this,' Hooke recorded, 'I answered that these sentiments were indeed worthy of his rank and reputation as it was known to the King of France.' Errol, whose grandfather had carried the king's sword at the coronation of Charles I, seemed, in conjunction with Hamilton, to be the man for the hour. However, when Errol came out to Comiston the following day he had some home truths to impart about Hamilton. Although two-thirds of Scotland were Stuart in sympathy, and most of the nobility who counted for anything ready to raise their followers for King James when the moment came,

Hamilton, their natural leader, was an unknown quantity. He was indeed suspected of seeking the throne for himself; and while the Scots nobility would risk everything to restore their lawful King, they would do nothing which might give the crown to Hamilton.

This was the first Hooke had heard of the duke's royal ambitions and he listened with scepticism, the more so as Errol's antipathy to Hamilton seemed to grow as he spoke. Why, asked Errol, was Hamilton thought to be so important? He had no great armed following. Such as it was, they were presbyterians who looked to the duke's mother who did not see eye to eye with her son anyway. Hooke countered this by pointing to Hamilton's large following in the country. It is the duke who follows his supporters, said Errol heatedly, and his credit is on the wane. Then, backing somewhat, Errol conceded that were the duke less devious he would gladly acknowledge him as leader.

This conversation (as Hooke noted it down that evening) included no mention of the government measure, introduced not two weeks past to the Parliament which Errol and the Earl Marischal were attending, for the appointment of commissioners 'to treat of a Union' with Westminster. It was the war with France rather than any vision of an omnipotent Great Britain which had moved Godolphin, Queen Anne's Lord High Treasurer, and Marlborough, her Captain-General, to push for some sort of union. The appointment of commissioners was an essential preliminary. The seemingly impossible task of securing the passage of the measure through the Scottish Parliament was the responsibility of the queen's new Commissioner in Edinburgh, the ambitious young Duke of Argyll, in concert with her ministers there – the Duke of Queensberry (now Lord Privy Seal), the able Earl of Seafield as Chancellor, and the unpleasant Marquis of Annandale as Secretary of State. Feeling ran high against England, and against the abandonment of what was felt to be a thousand years of history by this ruling clique of ministers so adept at feathering their own nests. Even they despaired of success, and Errol and the Earl Marischal do not seem to have taken even the possibility of Union into their reckoning. By personality and influence Hamilton, the patriot duke, would keep up the opposition to union negotiations in Parliament House. While he maintained this stance, for good or ill, Scotland would keep her independence.

At nightfall, with Father Carnegy as guide, Hooke rode the three miles across the burgh muir to Holyrood, there to meet Hamilton. He was riding into danger. Not many years had passed since another Jacobite agent, Nicholas Payne, had his ankle-bones shattered by order of the Scots Privy Council to make him talk: in vain, since, he courageously divulged nothing. At this critical time in the affairs of

Scotland it would be a perilous matter for an Irish intriguer with a dubious past and in King Louis' pay to fall into the hands of the Scottish authorities.

Hooke's main concern was Hamilton's ambiguity. The Duke's initial answer had been to refuse a meeting, for the spurious reason that Hooke was not mentioned by name in the queen's letter which he had brought from France. When Carnegy had succeeded in reassuring the duke about the authenticity of this emissary from Louis who claimed to be his Tower of London acquaintance of sixteen years back, Hamilton had then sent Hooke a curious message. 'Come after nightfall to my apartments at Holyroodhouse,' he said. 'I hope you will agree to our meeting taking place in the dark. I will recognise your voice: I hope you will not have forgotten mine. I have my reasons for this and I think you will approve of them. Do not tell anyone of our meeting, and do not attempt to communicate with France while you are at Edinburgh.' 'As I was well aware of his mystery-loving and imperious nature,' Hooke recorded, 'I agreed to all this.'

As Queen's Commissioner, Argyll was in residence in the royal apartments on the south-facing side of the palace. On the floor above, Annandale had his quarters. The house of Seafield abutted on to the palace's southern tower. In the warren that was Holyrood there were many who would be curious about the Duke of Hamilton's visitors: and it would be doubly unsafe for a catholic priest, albeit incognito, to take Hooke into the palace. Father Carnegy left him with Lady Largo (to give her the courtesy title of the wife of the Durhame Laird of Largo) at her house nearby off the Canongate; elderly, and although a catholic, she was the Duke's trusted confidante (unlike the other old lady, the devout Duchess Anne in her great house in pleasant Clydesdale). Across the outer courtyard of the palace, past the scarlet-coated sentries at the main entrance, up the interior staircase with its finely-wrought ironwork ascending to the duke's apartments on the principal floor, the old lady led Hooke to the door of the duke's bedroom; and there she left him.

In the darkness the duke was awaiting his visitor. 'He embraced me warmly,' Hooke recorded, 'calling me his prison comrade. I knew his voice at once.' Hamilton launched into excuse for the extraordinary nature of this meeting. He could trust no one, he said. All his friends who knew about Hooke would be asking if he, the Duke, had seen the French emissary; and he felt it essential that he should be able to swear that he had not *seen* him. However, he wanted to speak freely, and so Hooke could tell him everything about the proposals he had to make. In the same way as he had responded to the Earl of Errol's opening gambit Hooke replied that he had come simply to listen to what proposals the duke had to make to him.

Next morning Hooke, with his sharp ear and acute memory, recorded the dialogue held in the dark the night before.

HAMILTON: The queen [Queen Mary] seems to think matters to be in better shape than in fact they are. *She* cannot help us. Only the King of France can help us. I'm astonished that he did not send any troops last year.

HOOKE: Your Grace, the King of France has no need of the Scots. But has been informed that they wish his protection, and so he has sent me to Scotland to find out what they need, and to speak to you above all others.

HAMILTON: Have you a letter of introduction with you?

HOOKE: Yes, your Grace, I have a letter for you from the King of France, but since we are without light you will not be able to read it!

HAMILTON, (rising from his seat): If we weren't in darkness you would see from my face how moved I am at the honour the King of France has done me in writing me a letter. Please let me have it at once.

HOOKE: I will let you have not only this but also a document showing that I am authorised to do all that is needed for the good of Scotland, and for your Grace's own interests in particular.

HAMILTON, (after taking the papers into an adjoining room to read them by candlelight): I will cherish this letter in my family archives. The King of France has done me great honour in writing to me. I was ever the loyal servant of King James. I still am. There are many in Scotland who want him restored but they will not work together, and they lack drive. So I have to be extremely careful. A year ago I lost both a letter from the queen and the copy of my reply, and this has caused me no end of alarm. The Jacobites in Scotland frustrate me all the time. Indeed they worry me more than the English party. I have only kept my position by being flexible and by pitting one faction against the other.

In these opening encounters, Hamilton, as Hooke recorded, spoke with great speed, vehemence and repetition. There was, the duke went on, a great change in the complexion of Parliament. Some had gone over to Queensberry and the Court party. There was only one way to put things to rights. The votes of the burgh deputies had to be secured; they made up a third of the Parliament, and could be bought cheaply. With money he had brought from London, Queensberry was already buying the votes of some members from the north of Scotland to augment his own support. He, Hamilton, would be destroyed unless the King of France sent him money to keep his party together and win new adherents. This was the most pressing need. What had Hooke to say to that?

HOOKE: If the King of France takes Scotland under his protection, I do not doubt that he will send you money in accordance with what you need for the part you have to play. But you haven't explained how winning over the burgh members would serve the King of France's purposes.

HAMILTON: It would put me in control of this Parliament and so able to frustrate the plans of the Court. I would be able to prevent the question of a Hanoverian succession being revived. I would also make this Union project fail. Surely all this is worth some recognition?

HOOKE: Your Grace, I do not see things as you do. The King of France's interests would not be served by putting money into the hands of the burgh deputies. You might in this way successfully oppose the Court one year, but it would all have to be done again the next, and so the King of France would be put to perpetual expense to no lasting purpose. Now is the moment for *action*.

HAMILTON: So you want to incite us to take up arms. Perhaps we would like to do so. But we certainly do not want to start what for France would only be a military diversion.

HOOKE: If as you say the Scots are of a mind to take up arms, I can well see that they will require a lot of help. So you have only to say what you need. No one in France has in mind a mere diversion in Scotland; that is a calumny put about by the court in London. However, I must speak frankly. I think Scotland must turn the present state of affairs to her advantage and secure her independence and rights while England has such a great war on her hands and her army abroad. Surely the theft of the letters you mentioned means that you have nothing to lose.

How much you have changed since we last met! [in the Tower of London in 1689]. Then I had the utmost difficulty to persuade you not to take up arms, although at that time King James had expressly asked you not to do so. Now, when everything is favourable, you seem to blow cold.

HAMILTON: I have my reasons for that. I do recognise that this is the moment to shake off the English yoke. But I doubt if we could undertake to restore King James. Surely you don't think that Scotland could conquer England? . . .

Our aim is simply not to be enslaved by the English, and we think that if Queen Anne dies with the question of a Hanoverian succession not settled, it will be easy for us to break with England, or to make her accept whatever conditions we stipulate.

For all that they were conversing in the dark, Hooke's understanding of the duke's true purpose was now suddenly illuminated. 'At this point', he wrote, 'I began to see that Earl of Errol's suspicions were well founded, and that the Duke of Hamilton's sole purpose was to play things along until Queen Anne eventually dies so they may turn out to his own advantage. King James and all catholic princes are excluded from the succession to the throne by the laws made since the Revolution; and by the Act of Security the Scots have bound themselves not to bring in the House of Hanover after Queen Anne's death unless all their conditions have been met [by the English] during her lifetime. That same Act binds them to choose a king related to the royal house of Scotland, and this means that the Duke of Hamilton will be the only candidate who is not already excluded . . .' However, Hooke said nothing of this and simply asked if the Scots would be strong enough by themselves to resist the whole might of England.

HAMILTON: Scotland lacks neither men nor victuals, but we do need money, arms and munitions of war. France will not let us down, because it must always be in the French interest to set up Scotland against England.

HOOKE: Your Grace, you could be wrong about this. I think you should thank God that France's interests chime with Scotland's at this present time. But let this opportunity pass, and I can assure you that the King of France will not embark on a new war simply on account of Scotland.

HAMILTON: Do you think, then, that peace is near to hand?

HOOKE: I cannot say. But it would be unnatural that a war as fierce as the present one should last much longer. So I come back to the point: if peace comes soon, what will happen to Scotland?

But Hamilton would not be pinned down. Peace was not at hand, he said. Queen Anne clearly did not want a Hanoverian succession in Scotland, otherwise she would have sent to Scotland the fifty thousand pounds which was all she need spend to put the Scots Parliament in her pocket.

HOOKE: If she were to send down this money, what would become of you, your Grace, after all you have done to thwart England, her queen and her favourites?

HAMILTON: Many believe that Queen Anne has her brother's interests at heart, and that she wants to leave the Scottish backdoor open for his restoration.

HOOKE: Then, act accordingly, your Grace. Open this back door to your King.

Again Hamilton shied away from the point. 'I would like to do so.' he said, 'but this is not the right moment. It would be necessary first of all to win over Marlborough and Godolphin. I have taken some soundings of them and am sure that they are not as opposed to this as one might think.' 'If Marlborough took it on himself to champion King James', Hooke observed, 'then you would be nowhere. The English game seems to be to keep the Scots in a high state of anger so that England would have a good excuse to keep a standing army after the peace with which she might launch an attack on Scotland, so reducing her to the provincial status of Ireland. If that happens, what will become of your Grace?'

In that event, Hamilton replied, he would be ruined and have to take refuge in France. But this sombre reflection only led him to enquire whether Louis would make over to him the duchy of Châtelherault, the gift of an earlier monarch to an earlier Hamilton in the great days of the Auld Alliance, 'Which,' said Hamilton, 'by rights, is mine, though it would be a poor recompense for the loss of the forty thousand pounds a year which my son would inherit in England' [from the extensive Lancashire estates of his wife, the Duchess of Hamilton]. 'I put all this at risk', he continued apologetically, 'You cannot blame me for seeking assurances.'

HOOKE: Again you speak as if I had come to entreat you to take up arms. This is not my purpose. If I have pointed out to you the need for you to do so it is out of my old friendship for you – you who are now so much hated by the English. All Europe believes you will take up arms. You have already said that you want to do so. But if you are not going to act, we should drop the subject.

'This display of indifference on my part', Hooke reported, 'seemed to work as I intended it should. The duke jumped out of his chair and swore that he would take up arms when the time was right.' But then he slid off the subject, asking what was the Jacobite strength in England and Ireland. 'Surely, your Grace knows the answer to that,' Hooke replied: 'you, with your great estates in the north of England and your friendship with the Earl of Grenard' [in Ireland]. His bluff called, Hamilton agreed that, if armed, the north of England and the city of Newcastle as well as the north of Ireland would rise for King James.

Then, seeking to bring the duke's mind back to military possibilities in Scotland, Hooke asked him about the state of preparedness there. Hamilton replied that the Duke of Atholl had at his call two thousand of the best fighting men in Scotland, Grant of Grant twelve hundred, the Earl Marischal six hundred; though badly armed the county militias met to train every month, and the highlanders bore arms in their fashion. On his own estates he had arms for two thousand but dared not give them out because his people were disaffected. He went on to say that he and some other noblemen had recently sent money to Holland to buy arms, but the city council of Amsterdam had forbidden the sale. Edinburgh and Stirling castles, would come over, but none of the Scottish fortresses held much in the way of munitions of war. 'This is certainly the case,' Hooke recorded. 'Another nobleman told me that a Dutch frigate had saluted Blackness [the dour stronghold jutting into the upper reaches of the Firth of Forth] and there was not enough gunpowder in store for the salute to be returned.'

Seeing that the duke was now more composed, Hooke pressed him to say how many troops, in all, Scotland could muster for war with England. Thirty thousand besides the highlanders, he replied: 'But [still evasive] I do not wish to discuss this.' 'Anyhow,' he added, as first light glimmered in the unshuttered, uncurtained windows of the room, 'we are close to daybreak and so I must lie behind the curtains of my bed so as not to see you. But I will think about all you have said, and I would be grateful if you would put it down in writing. And come to see me again at ten o'clock tonight.'

The last hour was spent in gossip about the Jacobite court at St Germain. Hamilton, now concealed by his bed curtains, also read aloud from a paper he had written some years past on his claim to the Duchy of Châtelherault. At six o'clock, as a thousand serving lassies tended a thousand porridge pots in the high 'lands' of the city, Hooke stole away from the palace to Lady Largo's house nearby.

The meeting had been a disappointment. But that day the tireless Colonel committed to writing the substance of what he had said to the duke; and this he put in a letter to Hamilton which Lady Largo later carried into the palace. On her return she said the duke was impatient to see him again, and at ten o'clock Hooke re-entered Hamilton's unlit bedroom. This time he resolved to say nothing about restoring young James at St Germain to the throne of Scotland, the duke's purpose so clearly being to win the Scottish Crown for himself when Queen Anne's enfeebled body finally succumbed, as it surely must do, within a few years. Hooke's whole purpose was to stage a Franco-Scottish military diversion into the north of England immediately, which would force the English ministers to the conference table and so end this debilitating three year old European war. The problem was how to make the Duke of Hamilton's ambitions chime with the French king's strategy.

At this second meeting with the duke, Hooke began by repeating the fiction that the King of France's purpose was simply to help the Scots. He added that while Louis' friendship for James made him want to see the latter become King of Scotland in fact as well as in name, the King of France would not wish to impose him on the Scots; and so the best service which could be rendered to James was that the Scots should now take up arms against the English without there being

Slains Castle in the eighteenth century. From a contemporary

any mention of a Stuart restoration. In this way all parties might work together for the independence of Scotland.

HAMILTON: What you have just said is quite right. No other course will serve. But the foolish enthusiasm of the Jacobites spoils everything. They do not want even to talk of us taking up arms without declaring for King James. You would do well to dampen their ill-judged enthusiasm. Nothing would be easier than for us to take control of all Scotland, and if the Jacobites would only work together there would be no need of foreign troops. It will be quite soon enough to speak of the form of government or who is to be king when the English yoke has been shaken off. There would indeed be no difficulty at all if only King James were a protestant.

The fly cast here by Hamilton about the need to find a protestant who might aspire to the throne of Scotland was noted, but not taken, by Hooke; he merely replied that he would not quarrel with the duke's reasoning but that he had no instructions from his royal master about Scottish internal affairs. The duke now changed tack; could Hooke use his influence with the Jacobite peers in Edinburgh to persuade them that in following Hamilton they would ensure an eventual Stuart restoration? But Hooke saw through this; the duke's covert purpose was to dissuade the Jacobites from any immediate military adventure which could only destroy his hopes of eventually winning the Scottish crown for himself. Hamilton, increasingly frank as the night wore on, then said that the Earl of Errol and the Earl Marischal had come to see him not twelve hours past and that there had been high words, they threatening to abandon him if he kept himself aloof any longer. Then he fell to renewed abuse of the Jacobites for failing to follow him, even though he understood the true state of affairs better than any of them.

'I let him fire away without interrupting him', Hooke recorded, 'and then I said that I would do all he asked and report back to him how I had fared, but that I would not be able to give him the names of those to whom I had spoken.' This qualification put Hamilton in a rage. 'As my purpose was only to bring about a military diversion which would upset the Grand Alliance,' Hooke recorded with a diplomat's cynicism, 'I undertook to do all he asked of me.' As a parting shot he again put it to Hamilton that, were he to lose the support of the Jacobites, he would be defenceless against his enemies in Scotland and Queen Anne's English ministers whom he had so greatly annoyed. The duke's riposte was a reassertion that he could rally support in Scotland's Parliament if only Versailles would put him in funds to do so.

Hooke slipped out of the palace and rode out to Comiston. Again there was to be no rest for him. That same August day Errol and the Earl Marischal came to see him, and this time they spoke of the rising Jacobite enthusiasm of the Scottish nobility. They had, they said, enlisted the support of the Earl of Home; his feudal power extended over the corn-lands and grasslands of the Merse, and his standing among the more newly arrived Border aristocracy could bring out horses and horsemen in plenty. Yet another visitor to Comiston that day was the Duchess of Gordon; she was as encouraging, saying that she had learned that the catholic Maxwells of Dumfriesshire were ready to give their support.

At nightfall, hope rising that it might after all be possible to set Scotland alight without the help of the Duke of Hamilton, Hooke accompanied Fleming into Edinburgh, there to meet the Earl of Home, 'a man of about fifty, and of great probity'. From the earl's house, Hooke went on to the Duchess of Gordon's fine mansion high on the Castlehill, there to meet the Earl of Panmure. From the thousands of acres of Angus countryside they owned, the Maules of Panmure were wealthy by Scottish standards, their great new house the finest Scottish baroque. From this meeting and one the following day, the Earl ('he seemed to me about forty years old and extremely well-mannered') left Hooke in no doubt of his readiness to rise for the Stuart king. With sublime indifference to the fact of England's naval supremacy he said his preference was that France should land an army of thirty thousand somewhere on the south coast of England; in that event Scotland would need only money and arms. If, however, Louis wished to confine the Stuart restoration to Scotland, some six thousand troops disembarked on the shores of the Forth near Edinburgh would suffice. Loyalty to the crown had always been the strong suit of the Maules of Panmure.

Next it was the turn of the episcopalian bishop of Edinburgh, who stressed how important it was that assurances be given that the restoration of a catholic monarch would not lead to the re-catholicisation of Scotland. Like many others, the bishop pointed to the Duke of Atholl as the key figure, rather on account of the clanned support willing to do his bidding than of any personal popularity. Atholl had already learned of Hooke's presence in Edinburgh. Haughty and vain though he was, he was thought to be willing to be drawn into the net; his resentment at Queensberry over the Lovat affair still rankled. On being advised of Atholl's feelings, Hooke dearly wished to be able to send him one of the letters he had brought with him from Louis to pass off to the Scottish nobility as if from the King of France in person. But herein lay a difficulty. The remaining letters Hooke had with him were addressed 'à Monsieur'; no way to address a duke whom a monarch must greet as 'mon cousin'. Although Atholl could not be directly approached, contact was made with the Earl of Strathmore, a power in Angus from his great castle at Glamis; also with Lord Stormont, head of those Murrays who had found favour with James VI a hundred years earlier and been given Scone and its domains as reward. Both signified their support.

Some time in those days of late August, Lockhart of Carnwath met him. 'A mettle-pragmatical fellow', was Lockhart's verdict. 'In conversing with him it appeared he was a man of good enough sense, but extremely vain and haughty, not very circumspect in the management of so great a trust, being rash and inconsiderate.' What irked Lockhart was that Hooke seemed ready to pass by the Duke of Hamilton. He was also indiscreet, and had even asked to join the daily meetings of the Jacobite-minded in Steel's tavern over the way from Parliament House.

As August slipped by, Hooke saw an ever-widening circle of Jacobite-minded nobility and gentry. One disappointment was the meeting with the elderly Lord Aberdeen arranged in the Earl of Errol's lodgings. Like the Duke of Hamilton, Aberdeen was anxious not to *see* Hooke though he wished to speak with him, so conversation proceeded with Hooke in one room, Aberdeen in another, and Errol as go-between. Generally, however, there was enthusiasm for Hooke's message, though perhaps mixed with suspicion of his true purpose. All in all, there seemed to be enough Jacobite support to make Hamilton's shiftiness seem unimportant. Indeed, insistence that the duke should *not* in any circumstances become king seemed to be almost as much of a bond among true Jacobites as their devotion to young James over the water. But Hooke's dangerous presence in Edinburgh could not be kept secret much longer, and this put him in some difficulty since his instructions were only to negotiate with Hamilton. However, he asked that a representative group of Jacobite loyalists should return to France with him for effective negotiation with Versailles.

While all this was being arranged, Hooke was summoned for a third time by the duke to Holyroodhouse. This time the meeting was held in the duchess' apartments, she being then in England. It took place by candlelight – the duke had already sworn an oath to his friends that he had not *seen* Colonel Hooke – but with his poor eyesight and intense concentration on the task in hand Hooke in all probability took little note of the elegance of its furnishings. Bedcurtains of crimson and yellow velvet with velvet chair coverings to match; the large looking-glass reflecting the candlelight; the Indian screen; the tea table; the gilded frames of the pictures on the walls and their rich tapestries; the little repeating clock.

Again the duke set to abusing his fellow magnates. To a man they were untrustworthy, incapable, talkative laggards. Again Hooke had cause to reflect that Hamilton's real purpose was to discourage him from concerting measures with them. To throw the duke off the scent, Hooke in his turn descended to verbal abuse of Errol, the Earl Marischal, Panmure, Strathmore, Stormont and the others. This seemed to assuage Hamilton's anger. Recovering his genial temper he began to speak confidentially, as if indeed to an old friend:

HAMILTON: The more I think of it, the more clearly I can see how his religion makes it difficult to do anything for James. If he were to be restored to Scotland alone that could bring down on our heads the whole might of England: they would be afraid that he would seek the English crown as well. Yet it must always be to France's interest that Scotland remains separate from England.

HOOKE: I am sure it would be better that James be King of Scots and no more, rather than a king without a kingdom.

HAMILTON: But for the reasons I have given *he* could not long remain King of Scotland. It would be easier for a protestant prince with no claim to the crown of England.

HOOKE: I agree; and if one may judge the feelings of the English by what is published, they think that you are out for your own interests in all this.

HAMILTON: Yes, they do call me 'Stanislaus' [the then would-be King of Poland] and they are convinced that I am seeking the crown for myself. But they are wrong. My purpose is James' restoration.

HOOKE: And if you cannot bring that about?

HAMILTON: If we cannot do it, I would prefer anyone to be king rather than the Hanovers. James should not take this too badly. It ought to be a matter of indifference to him who has the crown, if he cannot have it. But where could we find a king? That's the difficulty.

Having led the conversation this far, the slippery duke again put the question which doubtless had been in his mind since Hooke's arrival in Edinburgh. 'If we make a king of our own', he asked, 'do you think your master the King of France would send help to keep him on the throne?' 'If you act now,' Hooke replied, 'Louis will see to it that Scotland's interests are safeguarded in the eventual peace-treaty: but if you put off taking up arms until the war is over, your chance of ensuring the permanent protection of France will have been lost.'

For some time, reported Hooke, the duke made no reply, as if he were in a dream. Then he said he was willing to enter into formal negotiations for French help to enable Scotland to break with England. Could he again see the colonel's authority to negotiate? But now even Hooke's patience was exhausted. Hamilton was leading him in circles.

HOOKE: Your Grace, can I see *yours*?
HAMILTON: *I* don't need authority from anyone. You are to negotiate with me in person.
HOOKE: I am authorised only to negotiate with those who have the necessary backing. I fear you are on your own.

This for the present pricked the balloon of Hamilton's pretence. He wrangled for a while and then conceded that, at heart, he felt that nothing could be done until Queen Anne died. Tenacious as ever, Hooke sought to heighten the duke's unease by pointing once again to the dangerous isolation in which he had placed himself. This Hamilton parried with an attempt to scare Hooke into leaving Edinburgh, and at once, before he fell into the hands of the queen's ministers. Then, at last, he grew jolly and said with a laugh, 'We've had some good arguments. Maybe some other time we'll agree better.'

So ended the third of these Holyroodhouse assignations with Hamilton. It was now clear to Hooke that they had been to no purpose. 'During the three nights I spent in his company', he reported, 'it was all endless argument. He asked for a hundred-thousand pounds sterling to bring matters to a break [with England], but he would not bind himself in any way, which brought me to conclude that there was nothing to be done with him.' Worse than this, the duke, if he could, would actively obstruct any plans hatched with the Jacobite nobility for extension of the European war to Scotland.

But Hamilton, it seems clear, had also drawn his own conclusions. Louis would not help him to the Scottish crown. As the Duke of Hamilton, with his wife's vast Lancashire estates in prospect, he had nothing to gain, much to lose from a Stuart restoration to Scotland and the English enmity it would incur. The time was now coming for him to desert the Jacobites and side with the queen's ministers. If that were to mean support for the proposed incorporating union of Scotland and England, then so be it.

Blind to the danger of Hamilton's impending defection, in his too ready acceptance of the prevailing view that Union would be impossible, in the last days of August 1705 Hooke sought to stiffen the resolve of the more committed of the Jacobite nobility. At the Duchess of Gordon's house he met an emissary come from Gordon Castle. This was Bishop Nicolson, Vicar Apostolic in Scotland, whom Hooke had known when they were both youthful presbyterians at Glasgow College. The Duke of Gordon was, apparently, firm in his promise of support, but the Earl of Home and Lord Stormont showed a disturbing tendency to speak of French invasion of England across the Channel as a condition of military initiative in Scotland. Hooke soon brought them to order: small wonder that Lockhart of Carnwath remembered him as a haughty Irishman. 'I asked them coldly', Hooke reported, 'to be so good as to tell me if they were indeed resolved to do nothing unless there was a descent on England so that I might so inform the King of France. This put them a little out of countenance, and eventually they replied that they did not stipulate it as an absolute precondition to their undertaking, but rather something which would make it easier to carry out. I contented myself with this answer lest I put their backs up [*les rebuter*]. It is always even more difficult to get negotiations started than to bring them to a successful conclusion.'

However, the Jacobite lords insisted on more time to bring to maturity the planning of insurrection, since so many had to be brought into the plot and they had to go warily; the suspicions of their enemies must not be sharpened. 'I accepted this reasoning,' Hooke reported, 'while pointing out to them that perhaps time was more pressing than they thought, that peace might come quite soon, and so their representatives would arrive too late. I also asked them to bear in mind that in November plans for the next year's campaign would be complete, and that I did not know whether the King of France would be willing to make any subsequent changes in these plans on their account.' In the face of this warning, the Jacobite nobles agreed to send across four representatives in October. They would sail in Scottish merchantmen picking up cargoes of wine from French ports – the Estates of Parliament in their defiance of Westminster having decreed that, war or no war, the Scottish gentry must have their claret. And so it was agreed: in October, the Earl of Panmure, the Earl Marischal, Lord Kenmure and Charles Fleming should go across the water. It was also arranged that before he left Scotland, Hooke should leave money with the Countess of Errol to defray their expenses.

In Edinburgh it now only remained for Hooke to have one last tilt at the Duke of Hamilton. With Lady Largo as go-between, he wrote to let the duke know that he was leaving for France in a few days' time. 'I also said that I wanted to see him so that I might try to have better success with him than previously.' Back came the reply from Hamilton. He would expect Hooke at nightfall.

It was by now the very end of August. In Parliament House, a mile away from Holyrood, the preparatory moves towards Union had been uncertain. This tangle of events was now given a sudden and unexpected *dénouement*. Settlement of the succession to the Scottish throne on the House of Hanover with the two nations remaining separate, *or* a treaty of Union between Scotland and England: these were the policies which Argyll as Queen's Commissioner had brought from London to place before Parliament. The first he had quickly found was unacceptable to the Scots. The second had made some headway during August but still seemed certain to fail. Argyll had the drive and the ruthlessness, and Queensberry had numbers at his command in Parliament, but many veered between support for the administration and opposition to its policies, reflecting in this the confusion Scotland now felt: a nation with an absentee monarchy, with ambitions which she could not fulfil, and independence which she would not surrender.

Meanwhile Hamilton, as Hooke now saw it, was playing with the fantasy that when Queen Anne died, the crown of Scotland might come to him, the 'Protestant' claimant. That ambition required avoidance of war between Scotland and England over the Union proposals. Equally it required that the project of Union should not succeed; but there was little fear of this happening while the Scottish Parliament, with so many members averse to Union, could be relied on to scupper any treaty negotiations. The spectrum of opposition to Union – from disbelief through dislike to abhorrence – would see to it that the Scottish negotiators would not be the tools of Argyll and Queensbury; and a Treaty of Union could only be hatched were the Scottish negotiators pliant to the wishes of the queen and her ministers. Yet the fact remained that for the administration the selection of the Scottish negotiators was now the sole obstacle to surmount. All depended on how Hamilton now acted. This then was the background to the last of Hamilton's Holyroodhouse encounters with Hooke.

They were still at cross-purposes. The one still sought an assurance of French support should he make his bid for the crown of Scotland when the queen died; the other tried to scare Hamilton into a break with England now. Still playing for time, Hamilton pressed Hooke not to leave Scotland yet. He refused to do so, and at last the duke turned honest; or as honest as it was possible for him to be. Hamilton had finally made up his mind what to do, though Hooke, faithfully recording his words, does not seem to have caught their implication.

HOOKE: I have only one thing to add. You have said you intend to take up arms [against England]: when will that be?
HAMILTON: At the right time.
HOOKE: When will that be?
HAMILTON: I cannot say. Who can predict the course of events? If they turn out happily, we will profit from them. But you can count on it that we will act when Queen Anne dies.

Then this duke without a friend, on the verge of a decision which would effectively destroy old Scotland for ever, spoke as if he must now confide in someone.

HAMILTON: Perhaps I will be obliged to support the measures put forward by the Court. ('But my purposes are still the same', he added. Complete frankness was not in Hamilton's nature.)

HOOKE: It is said that you have come to an arrangement with the Earl of Stair [acting for the administration] to this effect, but that your supporters will not follow you.

HAMILTON: I will act as necessary despite what my party think.

And there it rested. Hamilton now compiled a letter to Louis (with Hooke's help in translating it) and one to Queen Mary, and both were then enciphered in the duke's rudimentary code. Hamilton's last request was about money. Would Hooke leave a hundred pounds with Lady Largo and a hundred and fifty with Father Carnegy? Hooke demurred until he could consult the latter. Carnegy advised him to turn down Hamilton's request. 'For my part,' Hooke reported, 'as I did not want to give away the king's money to no purpose, I gave him nothing.'

The following day the duke, tottering on the edge of his great betrayal, enquired of Hooke via Father Carnegy whether he was satisfied with him. 'I answered that frankly I was not,' Hooke reported. Hamilton then sent Lady Largo to put the same question once more, and this should have alerted Hooke to the danger now imminent. 'I replied that I had promised to report faithfully all that had passed between us,' he wrote, 'that I would give my word on this, and that no one was better able than he himself to judge if the King of France had reason to be satisfied. Lady Largo who loves him like a son and, being a catholic, is a strong supporter of the right [la bonne cause] burst into tears. She said that she was sure that the Duke of Hamilton meant well but that his obstinacy and distrust had lost him all his friends and would finally destroy him.'

This final meeting with the duke had taken place on the last day of August. At the close of the day's business in Parliament House on the first day of September, many members having gone to their suppers, Hamilton, to the astonishment of lords and commoners alike, moved that the nomination of the commissioners for the Treaty of Union should be left wholly to the queen.

'This, you may be sure,' wrote Lockhart in bitter understatement, 'was very surprising to the Cavaliers [ie, the Jacobites] . . . 'twas what they did not expect should have been moved that Night, and never at any time from his Grace who had, from the beginning of the Parliament to this day, roared and exclaimed against it on all occasions; and about 12 or 13 of them ran out of the House in rage and despair, saying aloud, 'twas to no purpose to stay any longer since the Duke of Hamilton had deserted and so basely betrayed them.' However, those that remained opposed it with all their might and a hot debate arose upon it, wherein the Cavaliers used the very arguments that the Duke of Hamilton had often insisted on upon this and like occasions. What! Leave the nomination to the Queen! No: she is in a manner a prisoner in England . . . The Court [ie, the ministers] and the Duke of Hamilton . . . made few or no answers to the arguments against the motion.'

Seafield, the Chancellor and Hamilton pressed matters to a vote and by a bare majority of four it was carried. 'From this day', concluded Lockhart, 'we may date the commencement of Scotland's ruine; and any person that will be at pains to reflect upon the management of this affair must be the more enraged when he sees how easily it might have been, and was not, prevented.'

Reflecting on Hamilton's action, Lockhart suspected that the duke's crony, the Earl of Mar, might have 'bubbled' him, as he put it, on behalf of the administration. There were rumours – but rumour was the currency of the times – that money had changed hands. To the end Lockhart remained mystified as to the duke's game on that crucial evening; but Hooke's record of the Holyrood conversations shows that what had happened was more than hasty ill-judgement on the duke's part. In his over-eagerness to enlist Hamilton, Hooke had let him see that France would not help him to the crown of Scotland, and that his own interests would be best served by the union with England. An incorporating Union would bring no crown to the house of Hamilton, but in time there would be pickings.

As news spread of Hamilton's *volte face*, Hooke at Comiston was awaiting a guide to take him back to the north, first to Gordon Castle, then to Slains for re-embarkation on *L'Audacieuse*. On 3rd September he received an enciphered letter from Father Carnegy about the duke. 'His carriage the two last days in Parliament', said Carnegy, 'looks so ill that I know not what to think. I know he designs well but I am told he has taken wrong measures . . . To excuse him his friends say he did it in a passion, because his party would not go along with him in another overture'. Late that day another letter came from Carnegy to say that he had now received an explanation in the duke's own hand – no doubt his characteristically frenetic hand – of his about-face of 1st September. 'I went into the measure of giving the nomination of the Treaters to the Queen', the duke had explained, 'for if they had been chosen by the remaining majority of the States it had been yet worse'. And, anyhow, the duke airily continued, this talk of Union will probably come to nothing.

Hooke remained at Comiston for some days further for lack of a guide, and this gave him the opportunity in the early days of September to get in touch with Atholl by means of the Earl Marischal; and so, late in the day, Atholl's support was enlisted. But it was an uncomfortable delay, as Queensberry was thought to be on the point of instituting a search in and around the city for Jacobite intriguers.

On 5th September Hooke set out at last for Gordon Castle, his guide John Moray who had accompanied Lovat to Scotland in 1703 and was now a Lieutenant-Colonel in the French service. On the 10th they reached their Speyside destination, and here Hooke met the Duke of Gordon. 'He is so wholeheartedly for the King of England that I had no need to press him', reported Hooke sticking to the essential as ever. There could indeed be no doubt of the loyalty of this catholic magnate of the north who had honourably held Edinburgh Castle for King James eighteen years previously. He was a tall handsome figure, well-bred, well-travelled and with just a hint of ineffectiveness about him. 'Dresses well but is somewhat finical resembling the French . . .' was the description by another observer. '. . . loves his country and his bottle'. According to Hooke, Gordon 'said that . . . the whole nation wants him [James] to be King but it is necessary that a Protestant give the lead. He had pressed the Duke of Hamilton hard to do this because of his standing in the country and his religion'. Hooke must have winced on hearing this, the more so when Gordon went on to assure him that Hamilton was the only one to unite the nation for James.

Not that Gordon was for backing out. The King of France need send only ten thousand troops and arms to Scotland, he said. That would give England something to think about and force her to make peace. Indeed whatever the size of force Louis felt able to send, he would take the field with a thousand foot and two hundred horse, and those highlanders who would respond to his call. Pressed by Hooke, he said he could double these figures, with more to follow. The presence of the duke's lively and engaging son, the Marquis of Huntly, the swarms of Gordon gentry in attendance at Gordon Castle and the all-prevalent catholicism, made this a believable boast. The duke had also seen both McDonnel of Glengarry and Lochiel, the redoubtable octogenarian chief of the Camerons, and their loyalty was assured; Hooke need not undertake the arduous journey through the hills to meet them.

The sooner Hooke now left Scotland the better. By 13th September he was back at Slains, to a warm welcome from the countess and the news that *L'Audacieuse* had been riding at anchor under the castle cliff, but would come back as soon as the winds abated. Another five days passed before the little frigate could win back to the Buchan coast, and, during these days of waiting, letters from Edinburgh spoke of the continuing confusion caused by Hamilton's defection. The duke was still maintaining that he had acted for the best. At the same time, having learned of the plans Hooke had been concerting with Errol and the Earl Marischal, he was trying to worm his way into their counsels. But the disillusion with the premier duke was general; his purpose was now thought by most to be to obtain the crown of Scotland for himself.

On the 18th, *L'Audacieuse* returned, and Hooke was hastily summoned from his concealment in the house of the Keith laird of Boddom nearby. He found James Carron busy loading supplies sorely needed after two months of voyaging. Countess Anne had exerted herself, and before *L'Audacieuse* sailed with her passenger on the following day the frigate had taken aboard two beef-cattle, ten sheep, three and a half dozen hens and capons, twenty ducks, a dozen and a half of partridges, three great pasties, eight dozen artichokes, forty bottles of wine . . . But none of this can have been of any interest to Hooke as the frigate battled her way southward through rough seas. Throughout the week-long voyage, in the words of Carron's report, the colonel, poor sailor that he was, endured '*une lourde pénitence*'. He was sick as a dog.

With his report to the King's Council at Versailles, Hooke submitted a summary of his conclusions. Scotland was ready to respond to a military initiative from France. Most of her nobility and two-thirds of her people was Jacobite; the presbyterians were much less dominant than they seemed. Horse and foot could be mustered by the *grands seigneurs*, the clans could readily be disciplined into foot-soldiery as fine as any in Europe, and Newcastle (and with it the Tyne coalfields) seized. France need only provide a general to command, some thousands of troops, munitions of war and money; there was in lowland Scotland an abundance of grain, meat and *eau de vie* to sustain an army, and grass and fodder for its horses. All that had yet to be resolved was whether the French landing should be in the Firth of Forth from Dunkirk, or the Firth of Clyde from Brest.

However, for the present, Hooke's recommendations were laid aside. In the winter of 1705, as the war lumbered on, the king and Chamillart were set on a test of military strength with Marlborough the following summer on the plains of Flanders; a revitalised French army would emerge from winter quarters to take the field, avenge the disaster of Blenheim and bring the war to an end. This being so, it scarcely mattered that the Scots lords did not come over in person to France to concert plans, as they had told Hooke they would. The ship which sailed from Scotland in October carried barrels of salmon and boxes of 'Glasgow plaids' to buy French wines, but only Charles Fleming as representative of the plotters. Perhaps this was just as well, since she was intercepted by a privateer; and though Fleming was able to conceal the purpose of his voyage he had some difficulty in extricating himself from the Dutch authorities at Ostend.

Hooke also had much more than the Scottish adventure on his mind that winter. He was now promoting a project of his own; that the king should authorise him to raise a foreign legion which would attract catholic deserters from the armies of the Grand Alliance, thus simultaneously and ingeniously strengthening the army of France and weakening those of her enemies. However taken up he was with this, and with his brief return to domesticity (his wife having presented him with a son in December) he still found time to secure for James Carron the rank of *lieutenant de frégate* in the king's navy, which the master of *L'Audacieuse* so ardently desired.

Meanwhile, in Edinburgh, the reverberations of 1st September 1705 were still heard. Before the end of October, Father Carnegy wrote to Hooke in cipher via the pre-arranged address of a Rotterdam merchant. He said that the duke was now putting it about that his intervention at Parliament House on the evening of 1st September to give to the queen the nomination of commissioners for the Treaty of Union had been 'because he thought this would oblige her to choose him, who wou'd be a strong pillar for his country . . . and it wou'd give him an opportunity of talking to her freely'. On the principle that three excuses, however self-contradictory, are better than one, Hamilton added that if it was left to the queen to nominate the Scots commissioners, the Parliament in Edinburgh could frustrate the drive towards Union by complaining of her choice; and anyway it was all the fault of the Earl of Home who had managed affairs badly with the Patriot Party and riled him into making his dramatic intervention in Parliament House on 1st September.

Hamilton's elaborate version of events in this letter to Father Carnegy was indeed as tortuous as it was false. Lockhart of Carnwath had also heard from Father Carnegy the excuses the duke was now putting about and would have none of them, however much he wished to think well of his noble patron. As Queensberry's henchman, John Clerk would probably know the inside story. What to-ing and fro-ing, one wonders, lay behind the judicious wording of Clerk's memoirs? 'I knew', wrote Clerk, 'that this Duke [ie, Hamilton] was so unlucky in his privat circumstances that he wou'd have complied with anything on a suitable encouragement'. Yet he too was willing to give Hamilton's motivation the benefit of the doubt. Reminiscing on the duke's defection, he went on to say, 'He was not only descended of the Royal Family of the Stuarts, but under particular obligations to the Royal Brothers, King Charles and King James; however, he cou'd easily have been convinced that since the succession to the Crown of England had been for several years past, to wit, in the Regn of the late King William, setled on the Family of Hannover, it wou'd be next to madness to imagine that the Scots cou'd set up a separat King, or force any King on England but the persone already chosen by that nation'.

That was not the whole story, and the duke did not fool the Countess of Errol. In December she wrote from Slains to Colonel Hooke now at Paris; the letter, no doubt, crossing the North Sea by means of some trading vessel from Aberdeen or Leith to Havre-de-Grâce. 'There is now', she said, 'such appearance of a Treaty of Union as makes all true hearts more afraid than ever'. But the Duke of Hamilton, she went on to say, had been hoist with his own petard; the queen was not selecting him to be a commissioner and he was said to be 'in despair'. As always, it is a clever woman who can best understand a complicated man; and the Countess' final comment summed him up. The duke, she said, was 'ensnaired in the Union by the bait of a double interest'. It was his duchess' Lancashire inheritance that had done it.

# 4

# George Lockhart of Carnwath

In the winter of 1705 the Countess of Errol dreaded the prospect of Union: on the other side of the great divide in Scottish feeling many feared that it would all come to nothing. One such was young John Clerk, son of the laird at Penicuik House close to the slopes of the Pentland Hills. For the ability he had already shown in money matters Queensberry recommended him to Argyll, the Queen's Commissioner in Scotland, and Argyll agreed that his name should go forward for appointment as one of the Union negotiators. Clerk was dismayed. Not on account of his youth and inexperience, but because he believed it would be wasted effort. Clerk was later to write,

> This choise, however honourable to me, was very far from giving me the least pleasure or satisfaction, for I had observed a great backwardness in the Parliament of Scotland for a union with England of any kind whatsoever, and therefor doubted not but, after a great deal of expense in attending a Treaty in England, I should be oblidged to return with the uneasy reflexion of having either done nothing, or nothing to the purpose, . . .

Queensberry was insistent, and Clerk gave way: a great man's bidding was not to be resisted. In company with his fellow negotiators he arrived in London in April 1706. They were quickly down to business at the Cockpit, the court theatre of the great rambling palace of Whitehall, close to where stands the present-day Scottish Office, that child of the Union's middle-age. Queen Anne's London cast its spell on them. They were handsomely entertained, and for recreation even had a private garden at the Cockpit laid out for them. Three times the queen met them and the English negotiators, lending her considerable political influence to the cause of Union. With the Earl of Seafield as Lord Chancellor of Scotland on her left and the Keeper of the Great Seal of England on her right, seated in a great chair all gold lace and crimson velvet, in her melifluous voice she gave her 'ardent good wishes' for success and unanimity. Monarchy was still tinged with divinity, and when in May Marlborough overwhelmed the French once more, at Ramillies in Flanders, it seemed that the Almighty approved of Queen Anne, and that prosperity must come to Scotland from union with an England whose empire would expand with the peace which must surely be at hand. By July 1706, after a feeble bid by the Scots for a federal rather than a complete Union, all was successfully concluded. September saw John Clerk back to the pursuit of wildfowl and trout at Penicuik; and the Treaty of Union ready for presentation first to the Scots Parliament in Edinburgh, then at Westminster.

In France, meanwhile, the Jacobite cause languished. At Versailles, Hooke still sought to persuade Torcy that Scotland's resentment at the growing prospect of union with England was exploitable. He also kept up a cheerful correspondence with the Duke of Perth at St Germain; but there could be no concealing the let-down when, early in 1706, the belated arrival in France of Charles Fleming, solitary emissary from the Scottish nobility, appeared to be the sole outcome of Hooke's efforts of the previous summer. At the end of May the extent of the calamity to Villeroi's army at Ramillies became known, Versailles was dumbfounded, and at St Germain Jacobite hopes were frozen.

The *Régiment Allemand de Sparre* was at Ramillies, but far on the left wing and not engaged, though they shared the humiliation of the rout of the great French army. Hooke, now their colonel commandant, was not with them; he had fallen to a fever. However, later that summer as the floodtide of the victorious Allies swept through Flanders he was besieged with his regiment at the fortress-town of Menin; and when it surrendered and terms were negotiated, he once more met Marlborough. Or rather, from the detailed report of the meeting which Hooke subsequently sent to Torcy at Versailles, it seems that Marlborough sought out the Colonel. He was apparently all graciousness and compliments, recalling earlier meetings at The Hague and Aix-la-Chapelle four years before when Hooke had been employed on Torcy's errands; and he assured the colonel that he would see to it that the Dutch made no unnecessary difficulties over the terms of capitulation. Piquancy was added to the occasion by the presence of the young Duke of Argyll, a soldier once more, his stint as Queen's Commissioner to Scotland successfully completed. Also present was the Earl of Orkney, Hamilton's soldier brother. According to Hooke there was no mention of his own sojourn in Scotland the previous year, though Argyll must by now have learned of this.

Taking Hooke aside, Marlborough said he wanted a frank discussion about peace-terms to end the war. Recognising the high importance of the moment, Hooke was greatly embarrassed. Having been shut up in Menin for the past two months he had no means of knowing Torcy's mind about the continuation of the war after the calamity of Ramillies; and so he hedged with skill, confining himself to generalities – which, he recognised, did not deceive Marlborough – about the supposedly ruinous effect the war was having on English trade. He also excused himself on account of his own ill-health; and indeed during the siege his eyes had been injured by an exploding bomb.

The duke recalled their last meeting in Holland in 1702. 'When you met me at the Hague', he said, 'you spoke a lot about the Prince of Wales. Let us talk no more about his affairs. I can assure you that England is not interested, nor do I believe that either the Emperor or the Dutch would wish to side with him.' But the meeting ended pleasantly enough: some aspects of war could be civilised. 'I understand,' said the duke, 'there are two subalterns in the Régiment de Sparre who once were cadets in the Dutch service. They are now to be arrested as deserters. I know you would be pained by this, so you would do well to get them out of the way.' Hooke acted on this warning; and so were saved the necks of two young Scotsmen, one a Stewart, the other a MacLean, both of whom had come to Holland to take service with the Scots Brigade, and had then aligned themselves with King James, whom Marlborough called the Prince of Wales.

George Lockhart of Carnwath, landowner in Lanarkshire and (to use its old name) 'Edinburghshire', member of the Scottish Parliament and acolyte of the Duke of Hamilton, for a time becomes the main chronicler of events in Scotland. Lockhart's narrative, the *'Memoirs Concerning the Affairs of Scotland'* was begun in 1707 when the Parliament at Edinburgh, and old Scotland in general, were suddenly no more. It was written to assuage Lockhart's own grief and anger, not for publication; and so it is uninhibited. Its author was a man of honour, of family and of fortune, and as an historian his Jacobite bias was open. It is an indispensable source.

The Lockharts traced their ancestry back to the twelfth century. Mentioning the present young laird in his dispatches to Versailles, Hooke described him as grandson (in fact grand-nephew) of the Lockhart who had fought for the French king in the mid-seventeenth century civil wars of the Fronde, and had been both Cromwell's ambassador at Paris and friend of Cardinal Mazarin. George Lockhart's father added to the family's laurels as one of the outstanding Edinburgh lawyers of his generation. Until shot in the Lawnmarket of Edinburgh by a Lothian laird with an imaginary grievance he had been Lord President of the Court of Session, and had he lived would probably have been no Jacobite. His son, come to adolescence without a father, seems to have looked for one who would fill that role, and was befriended by the old Duke of Hamilton's dashing heir, the Earl of Arran. This was in the early 1690s when Arran was confined to his native land and country pursuits after his incarceration in the Tower of London for Jacobite leanings. Like Arran, the young laird of Carnwath became a devotee of the exiled Stuarts, combining Jacobitism with a sincere and articulate patriotism. When Arran succeeded his father the friendship persisted, and by 1702 Lockhart sat in Parliament at Edinburgh as a follower of the duke, one of his 'cavaliers'.

Like John Clerk, Lockhart was selected by Queensberry to be one of the commissioners for the Treaty of Union. By then he had married a daughter of the Earl of Eglinton, old Ayrshire nobility. As an improving landowner he saw bleak Lanarkshire responding to the new ways in agriculture, and his 'Edinburghshire' estate near Roslin was now yielding coal from drift mines along the banks of the Esk. It was not surprising that Queensberry as the architect of union with England should have sought to win over such a promising young Scot. In this he failed; all the while he was one of the negotiators at Whitehall Lockhart did not waver in his opposition to Union, even when, to wheedle the Scots into compliance, the English commissioners, as he put it, 'open'd their pack of golden ware'. Lockhart returned to Scotland resolved to move Parliament in Edinburgh to reject the abhorrent treaty. Surely, his idol the duke would save the day.

While stormy October weather lashed Edinburgh, sitting under the great oak beams of Parliament House the representatives of the nobility, landed gentry and burghs of Scotland had read to them the Queen's letter commending the terms of Union. 'The Union has long been desired by both nations', it said, with that bland disregard of truth which is sometimes a feature of the speech put into the monarch's hand for the formal opening of parliament, 'and we shall esteem it the greatest glory of our reign to have it now perfected, being fully persuaded that it must prove the greatest happiness of our people'. Then came a succinct statement of the case for Union, as persuasive today as it must have seemed to those who wished to be persuaded then:

An entire and perfect Union will be the solid foundation of lasting peace. It will secure your religion, liberty and property, remove the animosities among your selves, and the jealousies and differences betwixt our two kingdoms. It must increase your strength, riches and trade. And by the Union the whole island, being joined in affection, and free from all apprehension of different interests, will be enabled to resist all its enemies, support the Protestant interest every where, and maintain the liberties of Europe.

Edinburgh, said Lockhart, was a hubbub of political controversy as, by the middle of October, Parliament set itself to consider the Treaty of Union article by article. The Dukes of Hamilton and Atholl

George Lockhart of Carnwath by Sir John Medina. In a private
Scottish collection.

at once went into vociferous opposition, but the queen's Scottish
ministers 'very seldom made any reply, having resolved to trust to
their number of led-horses, and not to trouble themselves with
reasoning'. Godolphin, in command of the Treasury at Whitehall,
worked the powerful foursome in Edinburgh: Queensberry once
more the Queen's Commissioner, Argyll fresh from victory in
Flanders, the cunning Earl of Mar, and Seafield who, said Lockhart,
'was a blank sheet of paper which the Court might fill up with what
they pleas'd'. All were determined to bend Parliament to their will by

promises and, as was the custom of the times, by the extensive use of patronage. They would also be able to take into the reckoning what Lockhart did not know, or would not recognise: should it come to a slugging-match, Hamilton would pull his punches.

At this point the unexpected happened. The people of Scotland still saw themselves as the nation which had once bled for Wallace and followed the Bruce; now Scotland stirred. The suddenness of this rush of national feeling was partly due to the very secrecy in which the negotiations had been conducted; as the rumours grew about the nature of the bargain struck, Lockhart as one of the commissioners had put it about that the intended treaty was indeed a betrayal. While Union was debated in Parliament House, the opposition within was encouraged by a greater anger outside. Meanwhile Daniel Defoe, political pamphleteer and satirist, middle-aged businessman temporarily down on his luck, had arrived in Edinburgh in October 1706 with instructions to report in secret to Robert Harley, Queen Anne's Secretary of State in London, on the state of feeling in Scotland about the prospect of Union: he was enjoined 'to use the utmost caution that it may not be supposed you are employed by any person in England, but that you came there upon your own business and out of love to the country'. He too was now a spectator of the tumult in Scotland's capital.

At first it was no further away than Parliament Close, crowded every day, as Lockhart recalled, 'with an infinate number of people, all exclaiming against the Union, and speaking very free language concerning the promotors of it'. Queensberry was cursed as he passed along the street. For Hamilton, posing as a patriot, it was his finest hour; he was 'huzza'd and conveyed every night, with a great number of apprentices and younger sort of people from the Parliament House to the Abbey [his quarters looking on to the forecourt in the palace of Holyrood, where he had received Hooke] exhorting him to stand by the country and assuring him of his being supported'.

On 23rd October the crowds, after cheering the duke down the length of High Street and Canongate, went on to the house of Sir Patrick Johnstone, former Lord Provost, a member of Parliament for Edinburgh, a commissioner of the Treaty and a strong Union man, there to break his windows and, could he have been found, savage him. The house was a flat in one of Edinburgh's great tenements. 'The mob came upstairs to his door,' reported Defoe, 'and fell to work with sledges to break it open but it seems could not. His Lady in the fright with two candles in her hand that she might be known cries out for God sake to call the Guard'. (Scottice 'Fur Goad's sake, ca' the Gaird'). Defoe then watched the progress of this 'terrible multitude coming up the High Street with a drum at the head of them shouting and swearing and crying out all Scotland would stand together, no Union, no Union, English dogs and the like'. The tumult went on well into the night until strong detachments of Foot Guards were despatched to hold the Netherbow Port which joined High Street to Canongate, and also to the Weigh House at the head of the Lawnmarket, and to keep guard in the Parliament Close itself.

From now on, Queensberry, walking at the end of business from Parliament House to his carriage waiting by the Cross, did so through two files of muskets – 'as if to the gallows', said Lockhart; and his coach rattled off at a gallop with its escort of cavalry, under a fusillade of stones. But the wily Queensberry had the situation in hand. The small Scots army, all fifteen hundred of it, was encamped just outside Edinburgh; Godolphin assured the Earl of Leven at Edinburgh Castle that English troops would also be at Berwick, ready to march if need be. A 'Proclamation against Tumultuous Meetings' was issued by the Privy Council, the streets to be cleared at beat of warning drum and the Guards under orders to fire if it were not obeyed. Queensberry even contrived to turn it to modest advantage, representing to Godolphin that despite Hamilton's incitement the opposition to the Union was nothing more than the mischief of 'a parcel of rascally boys'. (It was indeed this same Edinburgh mob which had instigated the judicial murder of the Captain of the *Worcester* which Hooke had noted in the spring of 1705).

There was now a more general explosion of anger about the proposed Union. It came formally from the gentry of the shires. There was none from the fief of the Duke of Argyll or from those of the west country earls, Stair, Louden and Glasgow; none from East Lothian of the Dalrymples and the Earl of Haddington; but most of the gentry of the rest of lowland Scotland, said Lockhart, put their signatures to a document of dissent. From Aberdeenshire to Berwick, through Stirlingshire and the wards of Lanarkshire to Dunbarton-shire, Renfrewshire and the Stewartry of Kirkcudbright, they besought Parliament to 'support and preserve entire the Sovereignty and Independence of this Crown and Kingdom, and the Rights and Privileges of Parliament which have been so valiantly maintain'd by our Heroick ancestors for the space of above two thousand years . . .'. The same petition was widely supported by the inhabi-tants of twenty-six burghs from St Andrews and the other royal burghs of the Fife coast to Ayr, from Perth to Annan; and there was support in Edinburgh although the magistrates prohibited its signing.

November came, and under ministerial 'persuasion' the steady progress of the Treaty of Union through Parliament continued. The Dukes of Hamilton and Atholl in uneasy alliance; Atholl with his 'proud, imperious, haughty, passionate temper'; the Marquis of

Annandale 'much caressed but little trusted by the Cavaliers'; of the earls, Errol, the Earl Marischal, Wigton, Strathmore, Selkirk and Kincardine; Viscounts Stormont and Kilsyth; ten lords; twenty-five lairds and the same number of burgh members; this was the extent of opposition in Parliament, and in itself it was not enough. Towards the end of November, stirred by local Jacobites and the minister of the Tron Church, the Glasgow mob rose, driving out of town the Bailie Nicol Jarvies of the day who supported the Union. 'I am sorry to tell you', Defoe wrote to Harley on the last day of November, 'the war here is begun'. But rioting by the people of Glasgow, still only a modest town with four main streets and a bridge over the Clyde, was far from being decisive in the affairs of Scotland. At Hamilton Palace Duchess Anne, hating the prospect of Union but fearing mob rule still more, gave the Glaswegians only discouragement; and a detachment of dragoons sent from Edinburgh dealt with the insurgents and the two 'mean artificers', one an old soldier with Jacobite leanings, who sought to lead them.

By now there had been more unrest in the south-west. On the 20th of November, a force of several thousand armed men had descended on the burgh of Dumfries, there in public to burn a copy of the Articles of Union and hang from the burgh cross a paper setting out their reasoned protest. These were the Cameronians, the paramilitary wing of covenanting sentiment, as severe as they were warlike. In the formal English which Scots consider necessary for such an occasion, the Cameronians' declaration protested with dignity against the twenty-five articles of Union as 'nonconsistent with and utterly destructive of this nation's independency, Crown rights, and our constitute laws both sacred and civil'. It referred to 'the variety of addresses given into the present parliament by all ranks from almost all corners of this nation against the said union' and stigmatised the Treaty commissioners as 'either simple, ignorant or treacherous, if not all three'. If parliament ratifies the Union, it went on, and the extinction of 'sacred and civil liberties, purchased and maintained by our ancestors with their blood' it would not be binding on the nation of Scotland. Let right-minded representatives in parliament give due warning that Scotsmen will not become 'tributary and bondslaves to our neighbours, without acquiting ourselves as becomes men and Christians'. Lastly, and aiming at the regiments of the Scots army around Edinburgh and in Flanders, it expressed confidence that 'the soldiers now in martial power, have so much of the spirits of Scotsmen that they are not ambitious to be disposed of at the pleasure of another nation . . .'.

In the western shires, said Lockhart, the Cameronians were indeed eager to follow the Dumfries protest with armed insurrection. 'For

Queen Anne receiving the Treaty of Union between England and Scotland, 1706. After a contemporary drawing by G. Huck of Dusseldorf. Scottish National Portrait Gallery.

this purpose they had several meetings among the ringleaders of them, divided themselves into regiments, chose their officers, provided themselves with horses and arms . . .'; and in this national emergency 'were so far reconciled to the northern parts whom formerly they hated heartily upon account of their differing principles of religion and episcopal party, that they were willing to join and concert measures for the defence of their native country.'

Lockhart's hope was Defoe's fear. The Scots he saw as 'a hardened, refractory and terrible people'; there was a real danger that north and west would join in arms to overturn the Parliament in Edinburgh, 'to which they say there will be fifty thousand hands'. And Edinburgh was now full of violent men, many of them highlanders. In alarmed amusement Defoe watched them in their tartans with broadsword, targe, dirk and pistols striding the High Street 'insolent to the last degree'.

In Parliament House, meanwhile, the 'patriot duke' excelled himself:

What, shall we in half an hour yield what our forefathers maintain'd with their lives and fortunes for many ages. Are none of the descendents here of those worthy patriots who defended the liberty of their country against all invaders, who assisted the great King Robert the Bruce, to restore the constitution and revenge the falsehood of England and insurpation of Baliol. Where are the Douglases and Campbells . . . ?

This was a side-swipe at the Douglas duke of Queensberry and the Campbell duke of Argyll; but in the weeks that followed Hamilton defused the opposition to Union as effectively as he had thwarted it in Parliament House the year before.

James Cunninghame of Aiket was a north-Ayrshire laird of small means and limited military experience; he had commanded a company in Glencairn's Regiment, but the only operation in which he had ever taken part was the massacre of Glencoe, and his only appearance on the public stage had been his involvement in the Darien disaster. Now, said Lockhart, he offered himself as leader of the armed opposition to Union from the south-west. Lockhart, with two other Jacobite-minded lairds in the Scottish Parliament – Brisbane of Bishopton in Renfrewshire and Cochrane of Kilmaronock near Glasgow, uncle of the young Earl of Dundonald whose large estates lay in Renfrewshire and Ayrshire – gave him encouragement; and so the plan was set. Cunninghame was to raise the south-west, the highlanders of Perthshire were also to rise, both armed forces were to converge on Edinburgh; and at that point Hamilton and Atholl would step from the wings to lead the nation's rejection of Union.

The burgh of Hamilton was set as the rendezvous for the lowland insurrection. Then, as Lockhart recorded:

. . . above seven or eight thousand men well armed all with guns and swords, five or six hundred with baygonets for the muzzles of their guns and twice as many of them on horseback were just upon the wing . . . had not the Duke of Hamilton a day or two before the prefixed time of their rendezvous sent expresses privately, without acquainting any of these who he knew were conscious of the concert, thro' the whole country, strictly requiring them to put off their design at this time.

After this apparent fiasco Atholl's men did not come south of the Tay.

If armed insurrection was frustrated, there was still the hope that a reasoned petition to the queen would move her, and to this Hamilton seemed to give his strong support. A petition was speedily drafted and, as December advanced, Edinburgh was thronged with gentry from the shires come to support it — Lockhart says five hundred in all. Hamilton found difficulty with the wording. It must, he said, intimate a willingness to settle for a Hanoverian succession to the Kingdom of Scotland; otherwise it would make no impression on the English parliament. This amendment, inevitably and designedly, was abhorrent both to Atholl and to all forthright Jacobites. 'Whilst two or three days were spent in endeavouring to reconcile and adjust this difference', said Lockhart, 'the country gentlemen grew weary of hanging on to no purpose in Edinburgh, for many of them dropt off and went away to their country seats'. The Edinburgh landladies also seem to have helped save the day for Queensberry and the queen's ministers. Defoe had predicted of this thronging of the capital by country gentry that 'the dearness of this place where people now pay 2s. to 5s. a night for nasty lodgings will soon make them weary'. And so it did.

Nearing the end of the work which would extinguish it for ever, Parliament had now come to the 22nd article of the treaty which fixed the number of Scottish representatives at Westminster. 'Whereupon', said Lockhart, 'the Duke of Hamilton convened a good number of the most leading men of those who had opposed the Union, pathetically exhorting them not to look backwards upon what might be thought done amiss by any, but to go on forwards now at the last hour to do something to save the nation, just come to the brink of ruin'. He proposed that the petition to the queen be revived and that all members in opposition to Union quit Parliament forthwith. 'This', said Hamilton, 'would startle the English more than anything besides and convince them that the Union could not be founded on a secure or legal basis'. With Hamilton in this last Parliamentary roll-call stood Atholl and the Marquis of Annandale; the Earl Marischal and the Earls of Errol, Panmure, Wigton, Galloway and Selkirk; the Viscounts Stormonth and Kilsyth; Lords Balmerino and Belhaven; among the lairds, Lockhart of Carnwath who had wealth, Ogilvy of Boyne who had none, and Lyon of Auchterhouse who was a brother of the Earl of Strathmore. It was 'taken for granted' (the phrase was Lockhart's) that Hamilton would lead the exodus from Parliament House. 'All things being thus prepared and adjusted', he continued, '. . . it caused an universal joy, and great numbers of gentlemen and eminent citizens flock'd together that morning about the Parliament House to convey the separate members and assist them in case they should be maltreated as they came from the House . . .'.

Hamilton was equal to the occasion. He pretended to have toothache.

Some of his friends [?Lockhart] having frealy expostulated with him upon this his conduct, telling him this double-dealing and wavering would convince the world of what was said concerning his Grandfather [who had been suspected of playing a double game in the English Civil War] in the reign of King Charles the First, and he esteemed the second part of the same time, he was at last prevailed upon to go to the House and prosecute the measure . . .

When he came there he called for his friends that were upon the concert, desiring to know from them who they pitched upon to enter the protestation? They told him there was none so proper as his Grace, being the person of the first quality and most interest in the nation, begging and imploring he'd lead them on at this time, and assuring him they'd stand by him . . .

The Duke was not to be moved, 'though he swore he should be the first adherer'. So, the tragi-comedy came to its climax and in the wrangling that ensued the opportunity was lost.

Writing within a year or so of these events, Lockhart's sense of outrage was undimmed, the more so since Seafield as Lord Chancellor had told him that had Hamilton lived up to his boasts, the queen's ministers would have prorogued Parliament and abandoned the Union. Yet the wily Queensberry and his colleagues must have known that Union was safe enough. Patronage and corruption had done their part, and Hamilton could be relied on to do the rest. The inside story, as Lockhart had it (perhaps from Seafield?) was that the evening before this last chance to save Scotland, the Duke of Hamilton had a visitor:

The Commissioner himself or one from him (but I have forgot which) came privately to his Grace and told him he had intelligence of what was in agitation, and could assure him that if it was not let fall, England would lay the blame of it upon him, and he would suffer for it, and that this threatening induced him to change his mind and confound the measure himself had concerted, promoted, and engaged people of his principles to enter into.

The Lancashire inheritance was still at work.

# 5

# John Ker of Kersland:
# Colonel Hooke Returns

The Articles of Union had been burned with bravado at the market-cross of Dumfries. The Glasgow mob had risen. The potential for war in the south-west had been marshalled (at least after a fashion) by an Ayrshire laird. Atholl had raised his thousands. It had all come to nothing. With an eye to the attempted invasion from France the following year one wonders just how determined this armed opposition to Union really was. Was it merely a series of demonstrations akin to the petitions to the Parliament in Edinburgh from burgh and shire which, said Argyll, were only fit to make into paper kites? Or was it the very substance of rebellion? This requires a closer look at what happened.

It is clear that the raising of Atholl's highlanders was indeed incipient rebellion. Not surprisingly, with the general covering of tracks of subsequent years, there is nothing in the Atholl papers to illuminate this episode; but there is ample corroboration – as will shortly be seen – in the report of the government spy who was later infiltrated into the Jacobite camp, as also in Atholl's own conduct in 1708.

A hundred years or more later an echo was also preserved by that distinguished old gentleman, Colonel Stewart of Garth, in his *Sketches of the Highlanders of Scotland*. The memory of his native Perthshire was that Atholl had indeed raised '7,000 men of his own followers and others whom he could influence to oppose the Union with England', and that 'with this force he marched to Perth in the expectation of being joined by the Duke of Hamilton and other noblemen and gentlemen of the south; but as they did not move he proceeded no further'. Colonel Stewart added a footnote that, 'a friend of mine, the late Mr Stewart of Crossmount, carried arms on that occasion of which he used to speak with great animation. He died in January 1791 at the age of 104, having previously been in perfect possession of his faculties . . .'.

The significance of the Glasgow riots as a pointer towards a more general willingness to rise in arms against the Union is less clear. The central figure was not Findlay, the old soldier of Dunbarton's Regiment who led the mob, but rather the minister of Glasgow's Tron Kirk who had influenced it with his exhortation to 'up, and be valiant for the city of our God'. Such sentiments were widespread amongst the presbyterian clergy. In September Hamilton's brother, the Earl of Selkirk, had informed him that Lanarkshire ministers 'are barefaced against the Union and prays heartily against it from their pulpits'. Had this fiery denunciation of the prospect of Union been kept up the general impulse to rebellion would have been intense. However, through discreet lobbying by the influential Principal Carstares of Edinburgh University the feelings of the Church of Scotland were now cleverly assuaged and its position as the national church entrenched. This defused rebellion, but it did not convert parishioners into active supporters of Union.

The Glasgow riots are also significant in that they brought into the open the unwillingness of Duchess Anne at Hamilton Palace to fight the Union *à outrance*. Throughout the autumn her letters to the duke at Edinburgh urged him to join his brother-in-law Atholl in opposing the Articles of Union, and her son had responded with suitable assurances. On 29th November she informed the duke that she was encouraging 'frequent rendez-vous' (? meaning armed gatherings) at Hamilton against the Union. Two days later Findlay's company of Glasgow irregulars descended on the town. The duchess ordered a strong guard for the Hamilton Tolbooth and dampened enthusiasm for insurrection. 'If I had not prevented it', she wrote, 'the same things might have been done through this shire as was done at Dumfries'. Anarchy would have been even worse than Union.

The efforts to raise rebellion by Cunninghame of Aiket, the hard-up gentleman from the parish of Dunlop in north Ayrshire, were indeed as serious as Lockhart made them out to be. Writing soon after the Union, Lockhart noted that Cunninghame had been given a company in the military establishment of new-created Great Britain, but said that he could not bring himself to believe that this was reward for any treachery to the anti-Union cause. In this his gentlemanly instincts seem to have misled him. Years later Cunninghame confessed to John Clerk that at the last minute of the conspiracy he had informed Queensberry of what he was about. It seems more than probable that Queensberry, so alerted to the danger, then leant heavily on Hamilton to force him into countermanding the march on the key fortress of Stirling which would have united the armed strength of the south-west with that of the north and 'raised' the Parliament in Edinburgh as a dog would raise a pheasant. There was little likelihood that in that event the small army in Scotland would have been any obstacle for, as Defoe warned Harley in the November of 1707, the few troops they have there are not to be depended upon – I have this confesst by men of the best judgement – the officers are good but even the officers own they dare not answer for their men.

Lastly there were the Cameronians of Dumfries and Galloway, that loose federation of extremist presbyterian sects. It was they who would provide the link with the invasion attempt to come; and their self-appointed leader, John Ker of Kersland, would outdo Simon Fraser, the Duke of Hamilton, Cunninghame of Aiket or Colonel Hooke in deception and double-dealing.

Ker of Kersland was another Ayrshire gentleman of dwindling fortune. Twenty years later, grandiose business ventures in ruins and pursued by creditors, he published the tale of his part in the making of the Union.

He came of an old Ayrshire family, the Crawfurds of Crawfurdland in the parish of Kilmarnock. An ancestor had died at Flodden. More to the point, the then laird of Crawfurdland had fought with the Covenanters at Bothwell Brig in 1679 when the royal army routed the rebels; and in the years that followed he was harrassed by government. In changing his name from Crawfurd to Ker of Kersland, this grandson of a covenanting laird had improved still further his ability to be a leader of the fanatics of the south-west. The Kers of neighbouring Kersland, who looked back five centuries to anglo-norman ancestry, likewise had a strong covenanting pedigree; and it was the death in battle in Flanders of Major Daniel Ker of Kersland of the Cameronian Regiment which had brought about the change of name, Crawfurd having married the major's sister.

In the autumn of 1706, when Queensberry learned in Edinburgh that there were rumours from the south-west of armed insurrection in concert with the Jacobites from north of the Tay, he hit on Ker of Kersland as his instrument to foil their plans and had him sent for. The estate of Kersland was now encumbered with debt; its laird would be pliant. According to Ker the duke told him that 'Britain would become a field of blood' if this dual insurrection took place, for the French would be quick to fuel the blaze. The protestant religion, even the liberties of all Europe, would be at risk. But he, Ker of Kersland, had it in his power to hold back the Cameronians. If they did not rise the Jacobites would not stir. At this Ker disclaimed any power over the Cameronians, but the duke would have none of it, pointing out that his predecessors 'had commanded them many years and that I was the only likely person to prevail with them to decline such desperate resolutions'. Ker let himself be coaxed into the duke's stratagems. He refused payment for his services (he said) but asked only for the

J. var Gucht Sc.                    Hammond Pinx.

ANNE, R.

*W*Hereas, we are fully sensible of the Fidelity and Loyalty of JOHN KER, of Kersland Esq; and of the Services he hath performed to Us, and Our Government: WE therefore grant him this Our Royal Leave and Licence, to keep Company and Associate himself with such as are disaffected to Us and Our Government, in such Way or Manner as he shall judge most for Our Service. Given under Our Royal Hand, at Our Castle of Windsor, the 7th of July 1707, and of Our Reign the Sixth Year.

THE

# MEMOIRS

OF

*John Ker,* of *Kersland* in *North Britain* Esq;

CONTAINING

His Secret Transactions and Negotiations in *Scotland, England,* the COURTS of *Vienna, Hanover,* and other Foreign Parts.

WITH

An ACCOUNT of the Rise and Progress of the *Ostend* Company in the *Austrian Netherlands.*

Published by Himself.

*We should not regard any of our Fellow-Subjects as Whigs or Tories: But should make the Man of* Merit *our Friend, and the* Villain *our Enemy.*

ADDISON'S *Sp. A.* Nº 125.

*LONDON:*

Printed in the YEAR M.DCC.XXVI.

*Facing,* John Ker of Kersland. Frontispiece to his *Memoirs. Above,* Ker of Kersland's 'licence to spy' as reproduced in his *Memoirs.*

protection of a warrant under the queen's hand, should he now as *agent-provocateur* have to feign rebellion.

Ker then set out for Sanquhar among the hills of Nithsdale where the Cameronians were assembling from the burgh-towns and moorland farms of the south-west. There he persuaded them to accept him as leader; and from Sanquhar they marched on Dumfries for the burning of the Articles of Union at the Market Cross, 'by a considerable party of horse and foot under arms with sound of trumpet and beat of drum' – and with a bonfire made of the timber lying to hand for the building of the burgh's new steeple.

Ker now sent a secret dispatch to Queensberry about his achievement. Did the duke, one wonders, shudder at its suggestion that, 'it might be found expedient to burn the houses of some that have been most instrumental in carrying out the Union'; Queensberry's baroque palace of Drumlanrig was no great distance from Sanquhar. Having put himself at the head of the Cameronians, Ker now tacked about, warning his followers that the Jacobites 'who had all along been our avowed enemies and thirsted after our blood in the reigns of King Charles and King James were but drawing us into a snare'. Cameronian strength on its own, he told them, would be sufficient to outface the small Scots army and overawe parliament in Edinburgh when the time came – which was not just yet. Thus the great conspiracy was frustrated. Queensberry was duly grateful and hinted at favours to come. 'And so,' said Ker, 'I was led into further labyrinths'.

In his Memoir, written a score of years after the event in a vain attempt to wheedle money out of government, Ker took all the credit to himself for stifling rebellion in Scotland, and made no mention of Lockhart of Carnwath or Cunninghame of Aiket. Neither did Lockhart in his *Affairs of Scotland* make any mention of Ker, whom he later described as a man of low morals and total untrustworthiness. But Ker did play an important part and confirmation of this lies in Defoe's letters to Harley, for Defoe seems to have been closely involved with Queensberry in the foisting of Ker on the Cameronians. The truth seems to be that Ker did succeed in 'turning' one of the Cameronian sects, that which dominated the hills of upper Nithsdale, but that Cunninghame's activities were of much greater importance both in stirring up the south-west and, through his own defection, nipping rebellion in the bud. This however is a side issue. The important point is that Ker, by professing to lead all the Cameronians in armed opposition to Union, had persuaded the Jacobites that south and west of the Clyde there were allies for their cause.

With Union now a fact and the Scots Parliament no more, in the spring months of 1707 Queensberry made ready for his triumphal visit to London where an English dukedom awaited him. One day in April, said Ker, in 'Lady Murray's garden' (the garden of Moray House, off the Canongate in Edinburgh) two gentlemen asked him if he and his Cameronians would 'join in a project which was then afoot to bring in the Pretender', for which there would be military help from France.

Ker again sought out his patron. 'The Duke', he said, 'was much surprised when he understood a French power was to land in Scotland, and desired me to go into their measures in order to discover the Plot'. When his two Jacobite acquaintances sought him in his lodgings in the city, Ker told them that he would indeed be willing to raise the Cameronians for King James but insisted that he must know what assistance was expected from abroad, and who was to join at home.

Thus the conspiracy against Union entered a new and still more dangerous phase. For Colonel Hooke was once more in Scotland, seeking to harness to the interests of France Scottish outrage at the Union with England.

It was not so much playing the Scottish card as grasping the Scottish straw which led Louis, in the despairing aftermath of Ramillies, to order Hooke to Scotland with a cargo of arms and ammunition for Scottish Jacobites. That order had been quickly rescinded. However, as the spring of 1707 approached and confidence revived that French arms would prevail next summer in Flanders, Hooke was again despatched to Scotland, but with instructions to engage in talks about insurrection rather than single-handedly to foment it.

As two years before, contrary winds held the Colonel at Dunkirk; and when the frigate *L'Héroine* finally sailed he suffered torments on the five-day voyage to Slains. To help him in his mission, he was accompanied by Lieutenant-Colonel Moray who had taken him north to Gordon Castle two years before, in 1705. The voyage had been preceded by letters from Hooke to the Duke of Hamilton, in whom the court at St Germain retained its myopic trust. To Queen Mary, as to Middleton her Secretary of State, it was axiomatic that there could be no rising in Scotland without the premier duke. Nor, on this matter, was the young king allowed a mind of his own, although he was now eighteen.

When Hooke and Moray were rowed ashore at Slains from their little frigate, there to be welcomed again by Countess Anne, they found her clear in mind that Hamilton must be trusted no longer, and was indeed working hand-in-glove with the queen's ministers at Edinburgh and their masters in Whitehall. The same view was expressed still more vehemently by the Earl of Errol when he arrived at Slains after hurrying north from Edinburgh. Hamilton, he said, was not so much openly siding with the ministry as continuing to confuse his Jacobite following with all manner of difficulties. He was putting it about that Hooke had come too late; that the letters he had brought from St Germain were ambiguous; that a Jacobite rising now would be ill-timed. The general view was that he still sought the throne for himself and an ensuing Hamilton dynasty; nor was he forgiven for having thwarted the joint uprising that winter by lowlander and highlander which would surely have succeeded in putting a stop to the Union. The Duke of Atholl, said Errol, had now broken with Hamilton; and it was to Atholl that the Jacobites must now look for a lead.

As usual, Hooke was ill from the rigours of the voyage. From his sick-bed at Slains he wrote to James Ogilvie, younger of Boyne, the son of a near bankrupt Banffshire laird of ancient family, with a message for Atholl; to the Marquis of Drummond at Drummond Castle in Strathearn; to the Duke of Gordon at Gordon Castle; and to the latter's Speyside neighbour, Innes of Coxtoun. Privately he resolved to keep in touch with Hamilton whose royal ambitions might yet suit the purpose of France. The crucial question was now what support Hamilton had from the militant presbyterians of the south-west.

From the Duke of Atholl came the response that Hooke should make his way to Scone; to the conspirators was now to be added Viscount Stormont at Scone Palace, across the Tay from Perth. It was also arranged that on his way south Hooke should visit the Angus laird, Fotheringham of Powrie who was James Ogilvie's brother-in-law, Jacobites being entwined in bonds of marriage as well as conspiracy. At the same time Hooke persisted with his double game. He offered Hamilton the opportunity of a meeting; and he wrote to the Duchess of Gordon at Edinburgh who, though by birth English as well as catholic, was the link with the Cameronians. And he left a letter for the Comte de Ligondes commanding *L'Héroine* to keep to the Scottish coast for a while longer.

Travelling on horseback for four days – and, he added in his report, for four nights as well – Hooke came south from Slains to the Laird of Powrie's house near Dundee. The laird would have had him stay there; but keeping his purpose to himself Hooke was intent on getting to grips with Hamilton, and he could not do this from Angus. How the presbyterians south of the Clyde would act in a Jacobite uprising was more and more in his mind. At the Earl of Strathmore's castle of Glamis, Lyon of Auchterhouse, the earl's brother, mentioned that he was on close terms with Lockhart of Carnwath who, he said, had influence with the leaders of the presbyterians in Lanarkshire. Hooke responded at once by pressing for a meeting with Lockhart. By now another formidable presbyterian, a Lanarkshire laird named Sinclair of Steventon, related by marriage to the Lockharts, had made contact with the plotters at Scone.

Hooke's report as submitted that summer to Louis' Minister for War as well as to Torcy is lengthy and detailed. This was no mere verbosity: Hooke could be concise when he wished. But the report to the Minister had to persuade him that Jacobite resolve in Scotland was no illusion; and that however much Simon Fraser had fabricated evidence of Jacobite feeling five years past, anger against Union, against England and against the prospect of a German prince one day becoming king of the Scottish people was now bitter and nation-wide.

Furthermore, Chamillart had not been involved in Hooke's previous Scottish visit, and so everything had to be explained anew, and Hooke did not enjoy with him the same friendly bond he seems to have had with Torcy.

In Hooke's report almost the only significant fact he omitted was the location a day's ride from Edinburgh of the meeting he now had with Father Carnegy, Hamilton's go-between. Perhaps it was simply that he was a stranger in a strange land. Perhaps he wanted to forget how profoundly disappointing the duke continued to be. Nothing came of this encounter beyond some more verbal fencing. Hooke now moved on to Stormont's Scone, the great house built by a sept of the Murrays a hundred years past on abbey lands, where there were further interminable, repetitive discussions. Should an invasion from France precede or follow a rising in Scotland? How many French troops would be needed – five thousand, six thousand, or Hamilton's impossible stipulation of fifteen thousand? Feeling was hardening towards a military solution to Scotland's ills: and it was now or never. Nor did it now matter greatly that Hamilton remained aloof. At Scone, Hooke received a letter from the duke in his usual vein, professing that he 'would willingly give his life to have some discourse', that he would concur in all reasonable measures for a Stuart restoration but that James should not come across without a large army – and so, said Hooke, 'he wished me a good voyage'. Nevertheless the conspiracy grew in strength from day to day. The Marquis of Drummond came. So did Moray of Abercairney. The Earl of Linlithgow was known to be firm. Most important of all, the Duchess of Gordon sent a paper giving a declaration of presbyterian intent:

> The Presbyterians are resolved never to agree to the Union, because it hurts their consciences, and because they are persuaded that it will bring an infinite number of calamities upon this nation, and will render the Scots slaves to the English. They are ready to declare unanimously for King James, and only beg his Majesty that he will never consent to the Union, and that he will secure and protect the Protestant religion.

It went on to commit the Cameronian sects alone to raise five thousand men at once, and the presbyterians of the south-west another eight thousand. And it bore the signature of John Ker of Kersland.

It was this indication of support from lowland Scotland which finally resolved the Jacobite nobility and gentry to band together in a formal (and, as seen from London, treasonable) request to the King of France for military intervention. It need cause no surprise that extremist presbyterians should have pledged themselves to fight for a catholic king. As Lockhart of Carnwath explained in his account of the Union, they reasoned that the Almighty would surely in his own good time bring young James round to a correct way of religious thinking. It was the loss of Scottish identity they feared; that Scotland and her distinctive religious ways would be swamped by a wave of enforced episcopalianism. The south-west comprised the counties where, in folk-memory, the heroism of Wallace and the exploits of Bruce lived on. Wallace had been Renfrewshire born; in popular tradition 'Blind Harry' had kept alive the memory of his exploits in Lanark and Ayr; and Bruce had won an early victory over an English force at Loudon Hill in 1307, not far from the scene of the Covenanters' own victory at Drumclog. This was the countryside where in burgh-town or moorland farm lived on that robust view of the Scottish past which Robert Burns would catch and to which he would give such resonant voice. In these counties there was indeed a stubborn rudimentary patriotism – akin perhaps to that of the landward people of Ulster today. In having the Laird of Kersland provoke this dour people, Queensberry had sown the wind. It now seemed that he might well reap the whirlwind.

# Part II

## THE
## ATTEMPT
## ON SCOTLAND

# I

# *L'Entreprise d'Ecosse*

On the first day of May, 1707, the bells of St Giles' rang out over the huddled tenements of Edinburgh to mark the completion of the Union. Suddenly among the Jacobite nobility and gentry the arguing was over. No longer did they seek to stipulate the number of troops which Louis should send to help their insurrection. With Stormont the moving spirit, they drew up an urgent Memorial for Hooke to present to the King of France.

It began by recognising that Louis had offered his protection to Scotland in order to restore her lawful king; and so it was a restoration to Holyroodhouse rather than to St James Palace that was envisaged. In accepting that protection the Memorial sought to represent 'the things we stand in need of'; but first it referred to the new spirit of unity in Scotland and the fact that 'the shires of the west which used to be disaffected, are now very zealous for the service of our lawful king'. The promise – or illusion – of Cameronian support fostered by Ker of Kersland had helped tip the balance. This was less remarkable than it seems today. The Duke of Atholl who would take command of lowlander and highlander alike was a staunch calvinist; and moderate catholics and protestants perhaps coexisted more easily then than they would do in nineteenth century Scotland.

Essential for success was the presence in Scotland of young King James. On his arrival the nation would rise and an army of 25,000 foot and 5,000 horse and dragoons be quickly formed, having its rendezvous at Perth for the highlanders and those from the north-east and at Stirling, Dumfries and at Duns in the Merse of Berwickshire for support from the south of Scotland. The organisation which would be needed to provision this army was described in outline. Clothing there was in plenty – woollen goods were Scotland's main export – though 'of hats there are but few'. The main need was arms and ammunition. The highlanders were well armed, as were the Cameronians; but weapons, powder and ball 'also some pieces of artillery, bombs, grenades etc.' were needed. Experienced officers were also required, above all a general of distinguished rank to take overall command, with some senior officers; and while the nobility and gentry would be the colonels, lieutenant-colonels, captains and ensigns in the regiments of the new Scots Army, 'we want majors, lieutenants and serjeants to discipline them'. And money was needed: 100,000 pistoles right away to finance the march into England and, thereafter a regular monthly subsidy.

As to military support, the Memorial left the size of this to the judgement of the King of France, as Hooke had insisted it must do. The force sent should be large enough to hold out against the two thousand of Queen Anne's Scots army and whatever English regiments might come across the border. The size of the accompanying French force should also depend on the place of landing selected. On that and the timing of the rising the memorial prudently said that Colonel Hooke would convey the memorialists' views. The choices were Kirkcudbright, if the invasion force sailed from Brest; Montrose or the Firth of Forth if it came from Dunkirk. The month suggested was September 1707, only four months ahead.

Last of all it said with dignity,

In the pursuit of this great design, we are resolved mutually to bind ourselves by the strictest and most sacred ties, to assist one another in this common cause, to forget all family differences, and to concur sincerely and with all our hearts, without jealousy or distrust, like men of honour, in so just and glorious an enterprise.

Thus, within a week of the Union coming into effect the instrument which should bring it down had been fashioned.

For the rest of May Hooke busied himself in collecting signatures. First to sign was Stormont, who signed also for Atholl, the Earls of Nithsdale, Traquair, Galloway, and the new young Earl of Home, and for Lords Kenmure, Nairne, Sinclair, Semple and Oliphant; also for a great many gentry of the south of Scotland. At Drummond Castle the Marquis of Drummond signed, also on behalf of the chiefs of the Jacobite clans. Lord Kinnaird signed, refusing to see who else had signed, saying that what he did was from a principle of duty. Moray of Abercairney and other lairds from around Strathearn also subscribed. That wily and aged chief, the Earl of Breadalbane in his fastness of Balloch Castle in Strathtay, would not sign but he gave his support. Then Hooke travelled on to Glamis where the Earl of Strathmore signed for himself and for the Earls of Wigton and Linlithgow; and there the Earl's brother, Lyon of Auchterhouse, signed for himself and for Lockhart of Carnwath. On to the great new

Two pages (*over*) from the original manuscript of the *Correspondence of Colonel Nathaniel Hooke*: the credentials from the Scots nobility of James Ogilvie of Boyne, come to France to assist the invasion planning. This also praises Colonel Hooke's conduct in Scotland. The marginal writing is Hooke's (Pages 357 and 358 of *MS Add D.26* in the Bodleian Library, Oxford).

357. 1707.

Lettre Du 23. aout
1707.

Venez quand il vous plaira et a tel port que vous voudrez
vous serez bien reçu; mais si vous ne venez pas bientôt,
ou si vous n'envoyez pas dans peu une asurance de secours
le park se rompra et il ne sera plus tems.

An Original.

A Copy of
Boyns Credentials in M. Amats hand
given me by Boyn; att
Fontainebleau
Sep. 21. 1707

We Your Majesties most dutyfull &
Loyal Subjects Subscriving do in the first place return
our most humble, and hearty thanks for the gracious Mes=
=sage Sent us by the Honorable Colonel Hooke,
and in the next place we beg leave to make all du=
=tyfull aknowledgement to his most Christian Majesty
for the generous offers of the Saison en order to restore
Your Majestie to the Throne of your Royal
Ancestors, being fully convinced of your undoubted right
thereto, and of the happynesh we shall enjoy when it shall
please the Allmighty God to Crown your endeavours with
the design'd Sucessh. We cannot but recommend the above
named Colonel Hooke to your Majestys favour, when
we consider how prudently, and faithfully he has managed
the trust reposed in him, by your Majestie and the most
Christian King. We think our Selves in duty bound to
send James Ogilvie of Boyn to whom we give full
power to treat with your Majestie, and The Most

Christian King, what May be ye most proper ways & means to effectuate so great and Glorious a design, and to sollicite the speedy execution of it, We have already condescended on such particulars relating thereto, as did occurr to us att the time in the Memorial we gave ye Collon, and we being convinced of the loyaltie & fidelity off the Bearer, remit to him to satisfie your Majestie and the most Christian King, in what may be omitted in the foresaid Memorial, or what else he may be interrogated about it. We humbly entrat your Majestie to accept of our endeavours since they proceed ffrom the Sincerity of our hearts and your Majestie May firmly believe that we will serve you with our lives and fortunes

Sign'd by    1: Strathmore.     4: Patrick Ogilvie.
             2 Pat: Lyon.       5: Tho: Fothering hame.
             3: Kinnaird.
dated May. 19. 1707.

1707.        350.

1. Earl of Strath more
2. the Earl of Strath-
   mores, Brother,
   called Auctor house
3. Lord Kinnaird.
4. S. Boyn, formerly
   Lord of the Session,
   Father to James
   Ogilvie of Boyn.
5. Laird of Boarie.

Boyns heads for a declaration
in Mr. Arnats hand, given me
by Boyn Sep. 23. 1707.

An Original.

More endeavour'd to improve the affection of our Subjects att home than to procure assistance from abroad.

Therefore Come only with a force Sufficient to Secure our persons att our first landing, relying for ye rest on the affection of our Subjects & we will send back the foraign troops hem soon our Subjects desir it.

Express his resolution to maintain the protestant religion and to leave the regulation of that Matter wholly to his first parliament.

Express his affection to his Subjects, ye priviledges of the land parliaments, and to the laws of the land.

Express his willingness to agree to an union upon

house in Angus of the Earl of Panmure, where news came of the sweeping French victory at Almanza in Spain, news which was the more welcome in that the victor of Almanza was King James' half-brother, the Duke of Berwick whom, it was fervently hoped, Louis would see fit to put in command of the Scottish insurrection.

At Powrie, the laird of Fotheringham signed for fellow Angus lairds. Then Hooke took the northward road for the hundred miles to Gordon Castle. The Duke of Gordon was pleased with the memorial and gave every assurance of his support; but finical as ever, he said he would not sign because it required the young king to expose himself to the dangers of war. On to Coxtoun Tower where the laird signed, also for the Earl of Moray at Darnaway Castle and for the laird of Grant at Castle Grant – this last a notable acquisition; he had once been resolute for King William. Again Hooke fell ill – small wonder with the rigours of travel. Recovered, he rode to Slains. The clear-sighted Earl of Errol protested at first that the Memorial bound the Scots to venture everything but placed no such obligation on the King of France; but Hooke prevailed on him and he signed for the Earls of Caithness, Aberdeen, Buchan and Lord Saltoun, 'and for the shires of Aberdeen and Mearns', also for the Ayrshire peer, the Earl of Eglinton who was Lockhart of Carnwath's father-in-law. Last of all the Earl Marischal commissioned his cousin to sign for him and promised '28 field pieces and two battering cannon which are in his castle of Dunottar'.

In the middle of June the King of France's frigate L'Héroine picked up Hooke and Moray at Slains and brought them back to Dunkirk. The sickness which had plagued Hooke in the course of his Scottish journey had returned; plunging through the North Sea, the little frigate had taken all of nine days to reach the Flanders coast. 'J'ai beaucoup souffert', complained Hooke.

Back in Scotland, the word which now filtered through to Lockhart at Edinburgh was that Hooke had given assurances to his hosts that King James would be amongst them before the summer's end. For Hooke, speed of action was indeed imperative; on the very day of his arrival at Paris he wrote to the two royal courts; to Torcy and Pontchartrain, Foreign and Navy Ministers at Versailles, and to the Duke of Perth and the Earl of Middleton at St Germain. 'I thank God with all my soul for your safe arrival,' wrote the duke in immediate reply; 'We were terribly allarm'd with news of squadrons in your way.' And to young Mrs Hooke Perth wrote a short note of congratulation on her husband's safe return. The Duc de Chevreuse, as Saint-Simon said, in addition to being the only intellectual Louis could abide was also Minister of State incognito for the prosecution of the war. A formal member of the King's Council he could not be: he did not share Madame de Maintenon's religiosity, and so she would not allow his appointment. But he was privy to all that was afoot, and the Army and Navy Ministers were under the king's instructions to keep him fully informed at all times.

As Hooke toiled in Paris through the last days of June in the compilation of his report it was to Chevreuse that he looked for advice on how to proceed. 'Burn this letter after you read it', Chevreuse replied. 'Have translated the letters to the King you have brought from the Scots nobility. Give Torcy the original copy of their memorial to the King, but do not show it to Pontchartrain. The King's Council will not be able to consider your report for another week yet. And bring along the highland sword you fetched me from Scotland'. It was not only the Minister for the Navy who required careful handling. St Germain was a sieve for secrets; young King James' court must not learn too much, and so Hooke kept Moray with him in Paris.

As to Chamillart, the Minister for War and Finance, he was in poor health with overwork generated by his dual role; and that month the new Iberian opportunities which seemed to offer themselves after the Duke of Berwick's splendid victory at Almanza were in the forefront of his mind. So July did not see the promised discussion of Hooke's report in the King's Council. Instead – as is the way with overworked Ministers – he asked Hooke to let him have it *en précis*. Hooke sent this by return.

But now Chevreuse took over the role of advocate for the Scottish project. On the 1st of August he and the Marquis de Callières, likewise influential in foreign affairs, met Hooke in Paris. There in a house in the Faubourg St Germain the plan was concerted and its prospectus adjusted. The following day the Duke handed this to Chamillart.

England was bare of troops, it said, nor did any fortress in her northern counties bar the way. The thirty thousand Scots who would be raised would be joined by 'a considerable party of English' and would be able both to subsist off the north of England and levy money as their forefathers had done in their war against King Charles 1. Newcastle and its coal mines were the objective, supplies from the latter 'so necessary for firing in London that the inhabitants of that place could not be deprived of them for six weeks without being reduced to the greatest extremity'. London had indeed in that pre-canal era no other source of fuel. However, the coal pits of the Tyne valley were not the strategic horizon. Mixing shrewd calculation with wild optimism it went on to assert that many in England would want to return to their true allegiance to young King James, that even the city of London might be taken, and that Ireland too was ready to rise.

Returning to reality it said that the conquest of England was not the real purpose:

> This single diversion will infallibly overturn all the schemes of the enemy. It will force the English instantly to recall the troops and ships which they employ in different countries against His Majesty . . . It will entirely destroy the credit of the exchequer bills and of the commerce of the city of London upon which all the sums employed against His Majesty are advanced.

With credit damaged, England would no longer be able to support her allies 'which will soon force the Dutch, upon whom alone the weight of the war will fall, to ask a peace of His Majesty'. And at the very worst, even if the Scots were driven back over the Border, it would be impossible for the English to send troops back to Flanders or elsewhere, with Scotland in a state of general disaffection.

To safeguard the assembly in Scotland of her new army King James should be accompanied by a force of five thousand men, preferably of the Irish Brigades. The Scots ardently hoped that the Duke of Berwick, the victor of Almanza, would have command. They needed gunpowder, mortars, 'grenadoes' and a siege-train – and six hundred thousand livres. To transport this force to Scotland a score of 20–40 gun frigates should be provisioned and loaded with munitions at the Atlantic and Channel ports, then concentrated at Dunkirk in September. The troops for the expedition should be assembled under guise of relieving the garrisons of the Flanders towns. Their embarkation could be accomplished within a couple of days, during which King James – but with only a small retinue – would arrive at Dunkirk.

The passage to Scotland should cause no difficulty. 'The enemy seldom have any squadron in the course between Dunkirk and Scotland, especially at that season, and the frigates may sail from Dunkirk to the frith of Edinburgh in two days, if the wind be favourable. The landing at Leith, within a quarter of a league of Edinburgh, is sure and easy, and the King's frigates would be quite safe there'. Should things go wrong, the southern side of the Firth of Forth could be laid waste to deter the advance of English troops. This, said Hooke, was the time-honoured response to English invasion. 'It was the counsel which their King Robert I gave them on his deathbed.' Lastly, the memorandum warned that if this opportunity were not grasped the English would continue the war until they had their way in Spain and the Spanish Empire, and the ruinous cost of continued war would overwhelm France.

This memorandum Chevreuse now put to Chamillart, Minister of War and Finance, under cover of a letter from Hooke drawing attention to the memorial which he had already seen from the Scottish nobility and gentry. 'It is signed', he said, 'by thirteen of the chiefs in the name of the whole nation, but more particularly in the name of thirty others who had appointed them their proxies. They are the richest and most powerful chiefs of that kingdom who must be well-assured of the enterprise they undertake as they thereby hazard their lives and their families'. Hamilton was not of their number, but 'this duke does not act sincerely' and *l'entreprise d'Ecosse* could go ahead without him. Lastly there were appended translations of the letters the Jacobite nobility had individually written to Louis and sealed with their own coats of arms.

And last of all, Hooke asked that his expenses be paid.

That summer Scotland awaited the summons to arms from the arrival of her king and his escort of French troops. The new civil service for customs and excise administration, largely English in composition ('the very scum and canalia of the country', wrote Lockhart with a landed gentleman's aversion to civil servants), began to establish itself. Some Scots made a killing; having imported goods at the cheaper duties which obtained in Scotland before the Union, they now sold to England at enhanced prices. But Scots with a feeling for their thousand years of history were sick at heart; and in between there were, no doubt, many Bailie Nicol Jarvies torn two ways.

Not so the Duke of Hamilton. Jealous that Atholl had been the chief signatory of the memorial which Hooke had taken back to France he now wrote to King James at St Germain, Hamilton's letter was forthright in its dissuasion.

As to the proposal made by Colonel Hoocke to give five thousand men, I cannot approve of it . . . no thinking man will demand less than fifteen thousand men . . . If Scotland alone was aimed at I should not make this difficulty about it; but it is not worthwhile to come for Scotland alone. England is the object, and although the Union has disposed the west of Scotland favourable for the King yet that does not remedy the other inconveniences or the difficulties with respect to England.

Make no mistake about it, Hamilton continued, there are few Jacobites in England; and now that Union had been concluded it was too late for the attempt on Scotland. 'Excuse what I am going to say', he continued, 'I believe you never was sufficiently alarmed at this pernicious Union'. It would have been all very different, Hamilton concluded, if he had been given the £20,000 he had requested to buy the opposition of the royal burghs to Union. Now, 'either come with a strong force or wait the will of God'.

The laird of Kersland wrote to Hooke in early August, urging him to come quickly. His memoirs would have it that he was feeding government all that summer with information, and that if he encouraged the Jacobites it was only to learn their secrets. This might explain the attempt he now made to have Hooke correspond with him in the simple cipher he had transmitted via the Duchess of Gordon (Hamilton was 'Mr Cloudy', Atholl, 'Mr Firm', Queen Anne 'Mary Tomkins', Kersland himself 'Mr Wicks', and so on). But his letter bears a different construction, for government whether in London or Edinburgh was now quite unprepared to resist an attempt from France. Queensberry was in London and Ker was no longer in touch with Defoe. He was in effect offering himself and his Cameronians to the highest bidder, be he Queensberry for Queen Anne, or Hooke for the King of France.

There was however nothing but mounting anguish in the string of letters now coming through London from the Duchess of Gordon in Edinburgh (via 'Mrs Roche's hous att the Two Bleu Spikes in Red Lyon Street near Lamb's Conduit'). 'For God's sake! What are you thinking of?' she wrote in August. 'Is it possible that after having ventured all to shew our zeal, we have neither assistance nor answer'? The Duchess of Gordon's anxiety that autumn was the greater because of the growing suspicion of Ker of Kersland's duplicity. In her letters to Hooke of that summer she had insisted that Ker – 'Mr Wicks' in her cipher – was to be trusted, even though, she said, some doubted his discretion. However, her letter of mid-November warned that 'Mr Wicks is turned a knave', though, she added hopefully, the militant presbyterians were still firm for King James and were seeking a new leader.

Equally concerned but for opposite reasons was Daniel Defoe, still an observer of events in Edinburgh. He had seen the general spirit of bitterness with which the Union was received, and in July he reported to Harley on 'the intollerable boldness of the Jacobite party'. He warned that 'unless some speedy care is taken to prevent their disorders the consequences cannot but be fatall . . . The Jacobites report their King James VIII will be on show quickly . . . and the forces here are so contemptible that if any commotion happen they can do nothing'. On 7th August, wagons with 'the Equivalent', the sacks of coin to compensate Scotland (supporters of Union in particular) rumbled up the Castle Hill with its dragoon escort. This, reported Defoe, only increased the general disaffection. The people, he said, 'call it the price of their country . . . [they] are incens'd by the subtill Jacobites and too much by some of the Presbyterian ministers, and they go along the streets curseing the very English nation'.

Two days later he reinforced his warning,

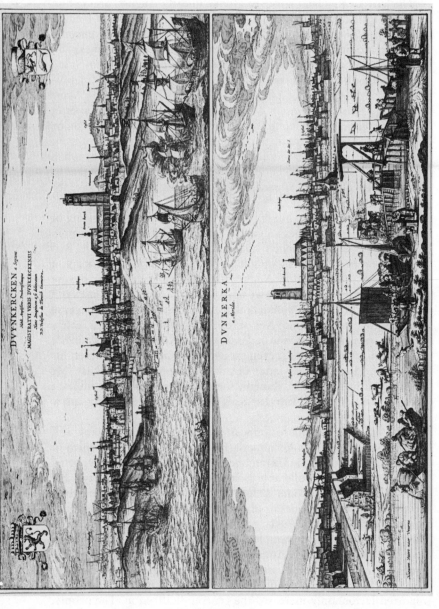

Dunkirk in the 17th Century before Vauban's reconstruction of the

I must confess I never saw a nation so universally wild . . . They are ripe for every mischief and if some general step to their satisfaction is not taken *I do not yet foresee how*, they will certainly precipitate themselves into some violent thing or other on the first occasion that offers . . . The very Whiggs declare openly they will joyn with France or King James or anybody rather than be insulted as they call it by the English.

The warning could not have been plainer. Harley is said to have shewn Defoe's reports to Godolphin, but there was no response. Political crisis amongst the Queen's ministers was now beginning to drive out all else.

In mid-September Defoe returned to the attack. The Scots were 'so encouraged by the successes of the French [Almanza and the defeat of the Allies at Toulon] and so unhappily back't by the common disgust that should the King of France but support them *not with men for they need them not* but should he send about 200 officers, arms and ammunition, artillery to furnish them and about 100,000 crowns in money he might soon get together 12 or 15,000 stout fellows and do a great deal of mischief'. If this money were dispersed among the Jacobite gentry, they would assuredly raise their men. In respectful exasperation, seeing more clearly than Harley, Godolphin or the Captain-General the strategic dangers, Defoe concluded,

I confess this would be a very fatall diversion as things stand here now, and I hint it because . . . it would be of worse consequence than ever with respect to other parts of the world.

At Versailles, in mid-September the plan for the Scottish project was read to Louis in council, and Chamillart assured Hooke that he would discuss it with the king later that day. Nothing came of this. Saint-Simon noted that Louis' distaste for the venture was the stumbling block. Perhaps he felt disillusion with Scotland. How could she have sold herself into subjection? Saint-Simon's memoirs may reflect the King's own views: 'It passes understanding how so proud a nation, hating the English, well-acquainted with them through past sufferings and moreover so jealous of their own freedom and independence should have submitted to bow their necks beneath such a yoke'.

In September a party, led by James Ogilvie, younger of Boyne, came over to France from the anxious Scots Jacobites. Accompanied by Hooke he had a meeting with Chamillart. The court had now moved from Versailles to Fontainebleau and there, as Saint-Simon put it, 'a certain vitally important project was knocking at every door to gain a hearing'. But still the king remembering La Hogue, perhaps remembering how he had yielded to Lovat's treacherous highland charm five years before and been deceived, still he would not bring himself to think about the Scottish project.

Only Madame de Maintenon could change the king's mind, but Chevreuse could not approach her, he being regarded as 'unsound' in matters of religion. Yet the Duc de Noailles could, and he was a friend of Chevreuse. By his intervention the matter was settled, and the king's wife was quick to see the merits of the plan. Her friendship with Queen Mary also made for a favourable hearing; at Fontainebleau that autumn there had been a visit from the Court at St Germain. Madame de Maintenon now spoke to the king, and Louis agreed, though without enthusiasm to the Scottish adventure.

But by now it was the December of 1707.

In the last days of December Queen Anne's ministers in London were given one last warning from north of the Border. It came from a Captain Ogilvie whom Harley, as Secretary of State, had sent north in October to report further on Jacobite feeling. Ogilvie's own Jacobite credentials were good. He had fought with Dundee in 1689 and then served with Louis' armies in the Nine Years War. (Had he been one of the gallant band of emigré Scots whose valour at *L'Ile des Ecossais* had so moved old King James?) Out of money, he was now a suitable tool for Harley's purposes. Posing as a Jacobite he first met the Marquis of Drummond in Strathearn, and it was here that he was given confirmation of Atholl's abortive rebellion the previous winter. Then he met the Earl of Breadalbane:

> After dinner when the cloth was taken away we fell to the same track that I had travelled with Lord Drummond. Breadalbane said he hoped for invasion in the spring.

On to Scone Palace and Panmure House, and through Angus and the Mearns 'where I found them all very ill inclined and want but an occasion to take arms and rise'. Then north to Banffshire of the Ogilvies and to the Duke of Gordon's country. 'There I found a nest of priests'; and so to the Earl Marischal's castle at Inverugie in Buchan, and then to Slains. Slains kept open house for Jacobites. One such was a Colonel Graham. 'He and I served formerly in France together', said Ogilvie, 'and we were long bed fellows'. Graham had been at Slains when Hooke was there. He recalled how the countess, though a protestant, had fetched a priest for Hooke's devotions; and that Hooke 'did travel up and down boldly as an English drover from place to place'.

Ogilvie said that though the Countess had been 'complaisant' with Hooke, she was suspicious of himself. However, Colonel Graham vouched for him, and her son the earl spoke freely of the mission to France to speed up preparations for invasion, and mentioned that a light frigate from Dunkirk was to call at Slains to warn them when invasion was imminent. From Slains, Captain Ogilvie rode to Aberdeen. There he learned that 'a Dr Gordon, a bishop in the Popish Church' had been sent to the Highlands to put the Jacobite clans in readiness. By December he was in Edinburgh from where on the 24th he wrote to Harley. He gave a clear warning of the dubious loyalty of the army in Scotland. Subalterns and rank and file alike had been subverted. 'If the P. of W. comes, they'll join him'. The remedy was to ship them off to the campaigns in Spain or Italy: 'As good they perish as better men'.

He also had a dig at his fellow-agent, Daniel Defoe. 'Nobody would suffer him in their company . . . for they believe he is sent down to be a spy over them'. However his report simply reinforced Defoe's repeated warnings to Harley. Scotland was ripe for Jacobite rebellion, and Atholl with his own seven thousand was ready to lead it.

## 2

# The Comte de Forbin

Since European war on the grand scale had recommenced in 1702, in the contest with the navies of England and Holland France's fortunes had been mixed. The capture of Gibraltar by England's navy and marines in 1704 and the battle off Malaga that year had given the Grand Alliance dominance in the Mediterranean. However, the allies' combined operation in the summer of 1707 against the French naval base of Toulon had been something of a flop. There had also been an upturn in France's fortunes in the striking success enjoyed over the previous two years by the privateers of Dunkirk and St Malo in attacks on ships of the allied navies and depredations on their great merchant fleets. For his exploits in this, *Chef d'escadre* the Comte de Forbin was now a national hero.

In 1707 Forbin could look back on service of nearly forty years to the days when the headstrong Chevalier de Forbin-Gardanne had been a cadet in the king's navy. He enjoyed the prestige of being naval attaché to the embassy the king sent to Siam in the wake of French missionaries, trade as usual following the cross; and despite his youth he stayed on to become Siam's admiralissimo. Returned to France, on the outbreak of European war in 1689 he served in the squadron of Dunkirk privateer frigates. That same year he was captured, but his hero status was inaugurated by his escape from custody at Plymouth and his crossing to St Malo in a commandeered rowing-boat. The story went round of Forbin's encounter with the Minister of the Navy on his unheralded return to Paris:

'Eu, d'où venez-vous donc?', said the minister. 'D'Angleterre', replied Forbin. 'Mais par où diable avez vous passé?' 'Par la fenêtre, monseigneur'.

Forbin had commanded ships of the line at the victory of Beachy Head and the drubbing at Barfleur, and with the return of war in the new century he was selected for independent command in the Adriatic against Austria. As that war worsened for France he was given command of the squadron of Dunkirk privateers. His were the qualities for the dash through the gun-smoke and cannon roar of an English man-of-war's broadside, to lay her on board, then under cover of a hail of musketry and grenades to lead the savage irruption of the boarding party – kill or be killed the only choices.

In the first year of his new command, while disaster overwhelmed French arms at Ramillies in 1706, Forbin's Dunkirkers captured two English line-of-battle ships, each twice the size of a privateer, and a score of merchantment as well. The king made him Comte de Forbin and a *chef d'escadre*; that is, a commodore or perhaps rear-admiral. (In character Forbin rewarded the courier bringing the news from court with a diamond ring "worth fifty louis which I took from my finger"). Then Forbin was off with his squadron to the arctic summer, there to strike at the Archangel trade from Amsterdam and the Thames; and in northernmost Norway, in the bleak anchorage of Vardo, he made prizes of seventeen Dutch ships. Returned to France he joined with the Brest squadron to win a great victory at sea with a combined attack on the fleet of a hundred ships which would have munitioned the English army in Portugal. This was the action which appalled even the battle-hardened Forbin when the 80 gun *Devonshire* 'was on a sudden all in a blaze before, behind and between decks, occasioned by the wind blowing very hard', and all but three of her people were lost. There was some criticism of Forbin's role in this action, and he may have been a difficult colleague for Duguay-Trouin, the commander of the Brest squadron. But Forbin was *aristo*, Duguay-Trouin was not, and with the intervention at court of his uncle, a cardinal, he sought further advancement. In December 1707 the Minister of the Navy sent for the *chef d'escadre* at Dunkirk. The king, he said, had resolved to provide six thousand men to escort the Stuart king to Scotland, there to win back the throne of his ancestors. Forbin would be responsible for their safe passage there.

In the drama of the attempt on Scotland the Comte de Forbin now moves centre stage; and so the trust which is to be placed on his Memoirs becomes a vexed question. It has long been established that the account they give of his privateering exploits are boastful and one-sided. They were published, probably written, more than twenty years after his retirement. However, with due allowance for whatever cussedness old age may have brought on him, the Memoirs do indicate the kind of man he was; and as it was his wilful nature – his Provençal *vivacité* – which was to wreck the attempt on Scotland, they are central to any undertarding of what happened. Had Hooke's own account of the attempt on Scotland not been impounded by the French government we would have a valuable cross-check on Forbin's narrative. But that very act of state of nearly thirty years after the event does raise the question – what exactly was it about the failure of the attempt on Scotland of 1708 by France's naval hero which had to be suppressed so long after the event? With all this in mind we may turn to the lively English translation made of Forbin's Memoirs soon after they were published in Paris in 1731.

On being told by Pontchartrain, Minister for the Navy, of his new commission, Forbin's reaction was to splutter that no good could come of it. Scotland was not ripe for revolt. Nor on her exposed eastern coast was there a port which could shelter an invasion fleet. If the king wished to squander six thousand of his army, would it not be better to sacrifice them in a sea-borne attack on Amsterdam and that city's conglomeration of shipping? Pontchartrain told him curtly to do the royal bidding. 'Le roi le veut', he said; adding, correctly, that the Scots only awaited the arrival off their shores of an invasion fleet for them to declare for King James.

This passage in Forbin's Memoirs is believable enough; it would have been in character for him to pontificate on the political condition of Scotland without knowing the true state of affairs there. It is also likely that his account of the audience given him by the king before he set out for Dunkirk in January approximates to the truth. The memory of that royal put-down would, one feels, be etched on his mind.

'M'sieur le Comte, you realise the importance of your commission. I hope that you will acquit yourself worthily.'

'Sire, you do me great honour. But if your Majesty would vouchsafe to me a few moments I would venture to represent certain matters in regard to the commission with which I am charged.'

'M'sieur de Forbin, I wish you a successful voyage. I am busy and cannot listen to you now.'

Royal dignity had been asserted, but had anyone explained to the commander of the invasion fleet its strategic purpose and the fact that this was France's last throw of the dice to recoup her losses in the great European war? Presumably not the Minister of the Navy who for his own reasons of private enmity was unenthusiastic about the project.

Another man of the moment in France with misgivings about the attempt on Scotland was the Duke of Berwick, the bastard soldier son of King James II by Arabella Churchill, and thus a nephew of the Duke of Marlborough though fighting on the opposite side to his uncle. Something of his uncle's genius for war glowed in Berwick, already in these closing months of 1707 a marshal of France. While still a boy he had fought with distinction against the Turks in Hungary. Before he had fully come of age he held command in the Irish war of the early 1690s against the armies of Dutch William, and in Flanders he fought for France under the great Luxembourg. In the renewed war of 1702 Louis selected him for high command in Spain, and he repaid this trust in April 1707 with his sparkling victory over the English and Portuguese near the old walled town of Almanza in Murcia. A French princess with a sharp tongue had described him as a 'great dry devil of an Englishman who always goes on his own way'; but he was now the hero of the hour, and France had been short of victories.

In the last months of 1707, as armies all over Europe took to their winter quarters, Berwick waited at Pamplona for Louis' summons, available for whatever new tasks might be put upon him. Spain no longer needed his presence; the English naval attack on Toulon that autumn had failed; and Berwick was intensely interested in the proposed attempt on Scotland. Sometime in these winter months Louis invited his youngest marshal's views on how this should be managed. Berwick's careful reply in writing recommended a landing 'at the river near Glasgow, with troops sailing from Brest'. A landing force setting itself ashore in the Firth of Clyde could, he said, quickly march on Edinburgh and Stirling, and thus seize control of Scotland. 'I cannot say anything about the problem of transport', Berwick continued, 'for that is a naval matter which I do not understand'. Nor need his memorandum be read as outright opposition to Hooke's plan for a descent on the east of Scotland with speedy ships sailing from Dunkirk. What it may well have been he wished to imply was that he, as James' half-brother, should be given command of the expedition. Perhaps he feared the inexperience of James who, in his nineteen years, had scarcely been allowed to stir from St Germain and the domination of his beautiful, bigoted mother.

Berwick was, indeed, the obvious choice for commander of the expedition, even though he was now formally a subject of the King of France. However, Chamillart, as Minister for War, wished the leadership of the expedition to be given to the Comte de Gacé, brother of a friend; Gacé would thereby earn the brevet of a marshal of France. Louis did not overrule him.

Why? Many years later, in his *History of the Age of Louis* XIV, with information given him by the aged Torcy, Voltaire wrote of the King's motives in assenting to the attempt on Scotland.

Success was doubtful; but Louis XIV foresaw certain glory in the mere undertaking of it. He confessed himself that he was impelled by this motive, as much as by political interests.

As we will see this is not to be swallowed whole, but if glory for France and her monarch was the prize, Louis may have felt that a Frenchman of distinguished lineage should have command rather than a 'great, dry devil of an Englishman, who always goes on his own

Le Comte de Forbin. From the frontispiece to *La Vie du Comte de Forbin* by M. Richer; Paris 1785.

way'. Or did he feel that, should the attempt on Scotland go well, King James' half-brother might not draw rein when (as might happen) it would be in France's interest that he should do so?

The decision having been taken to play the Scottish card, another imaginative, and linked, way to bring the European war to an end came into view. It called for as much secrecy as *l'entreprise d'Ecosse*, but again Saint-Simon was in the know. (The secrecy shrouding this initiative seems to have persisted to the present day. British histories of the great war of 1702–14 do not seem even to mention it).

Success in Scotland would draw off the British regiments in Flanders. If, as was likely, these ten battalions were not enough to stop the thirty thousand Scots swarming across the Border, Marlborough would surely ask the Dutch for help; and in the thinning out of their garrisons in the towns of Flanders would lie France's opportunity. The towns in what had been the Spanish Netherlands hated their new Dutch masters and were ready to revolt. In the first weeks of 1708 the Comte de Bergeyck, the Flemish nobleman who had been Minister of Finance in the Spanish Netherlands, was drawn into the planning at Versailles. He was told of the Scottish project and agreed that when the allied garrisons were weakened there would be a rising in the cities and towns of Belgium which France could quickly support, but everything depended on Scotland first being set ablaze.

Marshall Vendôme who now commanded in Flanders took part in planning the French army's part in this affair. Perhaps the staff-work did not quite match the soundness of the strategic concept; Saint-Simon has an anecdote of the great marshal and Bergeyck quarrelling in front of the king about how close Maastricht lay to the Meuse, Vendôme refusing to accept the word of a mere *homme de la plume*, Louis ending debate by sending for a map which proved the pen-pusher to be in the right.

The new year which began at Versailles with fêtes, parties of pleasure and balls graced by the presence of the young Stuart King from St Germain and his pretty sister, also saw the beginning of serious planning for the attempt on Scotland by the two Ministries, of War and of the Navy. To maintain secrecy nothing was put in writing, De Guay the Intendant at Dunkirk being summoned from there to receive his orders.

In his Memoirs Forbin describes how, single-handed, he now overturned the proposal by the Minister and the Intendant that slow moving transports should be used instead of the swift Dunkirk privateering frigates. 'Fairly letting myself go with Provençal verve', as he put it, he rounded on the two. The minister may have seen his role as that of limiting the inevitable loss to the navy, the sacrifice of transports much to be preferred to that of the successful Dunkirkers. The grand plan to bring the war to an end by means of twin popular risings in Scotland and Flanders does not seem to have appealed to him; and behind it all, as Saint-Simon reports, was his intense hatred of Chamillart. There is another aspect of this incident to note. In character, Forbin assigned to himself the credit for the employment of Dunkirk privateers in the attempt on Scotland. But for months now Hooke had been urging just that, recognising that much would depend on their greater speed through the water.

Twelve battalions from six regiments, the Béarn, the Agenois, the Beaufermé, the Luxembourg, the Auxerrois and the Boulonnais were ordered to Dunkirk, though to maintain secrecy they were held at Calais, St Omer or Lille, and it was given out that they were merely reliefs for the Flanders garrisons. Also at St Omer were detachments from the Irish Brigades which were to provide regimental officers and sergeants for the Scottish army, and to give that army a command structure, four lieutenant-generals with brigadiers and colonels were designated; also an engineer and an artillery expert. A M. Andrezel, a *secrétaire de cabinet* who had served in Italy as intendant to the army there, was instructed to take charge of the preparations for war 'which the King has allowed certain of his subjects to make at the port of Dunkirk'. There was some delay in that certain of the regiments had had to march from Brittany and Normandy; but all in all, said Saint-Simon, Chamillart, though close to collapse with exhaustion, had done his best.

The telling delay was in the assembly of five thousand sailors from Brest and the Channel ports to join the two thousand at Dunkirk who would man the score or more of privateering frigates and their five escorting ships of the line. To take command on each of the privateers, officers of the king's navy had to be found. However, by the middle of February 1708 all was nearly ready. To hinder the flow of information across the Channel the ports along the coasts of Normandy and Picardy were closed. Two light frigates now slipped out of Dunkirk. *Le Cigalle* carried Charles Fleming come from St Germain. *La Flore* in a duplicate mission had as passenger one of the Jacobite go-betweens who had come across in September with James Ogilvie. They were to tell the Scots to make ready: their king was coming.

Fleming had left St Germain on 18th February. The following day he set out from Paris on the great highway to the north: two days later he was at Dunkirk. An exasperating delay followed as he waited for James Carron, who did not come (we are not told why but there is a hint of a personal failing) and it was not until nightfall on the 25th that Forbin could despatch Fleming on *Le Cigalle*, no stranger to the

Aberdeenshire coast. Six days later, off Cruden Bay Fleming shifted to a fishing boat that he might slip unobtrusively into Slains.

This was cutting it fine. If all went well Forbin's invasion fleet would be in the Firth of Forth within a week. The Countess of Errol and her son were overjoyed; and the earl at once sent off a messenger to a Fife laird, James Malcolm of Grange, 'with orders', said Fleming, 'to have a boat and pilots ready to go on board the first vessel that should give the signal agreed to'. Malcolm was also to alert the fishing and seagoing burghs and villages along the shores of the Forth, from Crail to Inverkeithing, from Dunbar to Cramond. Their barques and boats would be needed for the business of speedy off-loading and disembarkation.

Errol also sent urgent word to the Earl Marischal to spread the news among the gentry of the Mearns who looked to him; and the Earl Marischal himself went into Aberdeenshire to 'the country of Marr' where he also had influence. Fleming alerted the Marquis of Huntly at Gordon Castle so that he might raise the Jacobite clans of the central highlands through to the Camerons in Lochaber and to Clan Donald beyond, and he also wrote to the Innes laird at Coxtoun Tower in Morayshire asking him to raise his followers.

On 5th March, Fleming 'was at my Lord Strathmore's in Angus and gave him the instructions of the King'. From Glamis the earl sent word to the Angus gentry and to that other Angus magnate, the Earl of Panmure. That same evening Fleming was at the house near Dunkeld of Lord Nairne, the Duke of Atholl's brother; of all the Jacobite-minded nobility it was Atholl who must take the lead. The duke who, whether by design or accident, had failed to meet Hooke in both his Scottish journeys, now shewed his readiness to come into the open. He was, said Fleming, 'in such a temper as we could wish. For five months before he had all his vassals ready to take arms upon the first news of the King's arrival'. There was however one shadow which Fleming could not quite dispel:

> He asked of me several times, and with great earnestness, the name of the general who was to command them. I found him, and all the other chiefs whom I saw, fully persuaded that it was the Duke of Berwick; for they could not imagine that he could be recalled from Spain for any other purpose, as he was a subject of his Britannic Majesty. They had conceived so great an esteem for him that I durst not venture to tell them that he was not to be employed in the expedition . . .

Lord Nairne now hurried southwards to Hamilton Palace to warn Duchess Anne.

Fleming, meanwhile, rode deeper into Perthshire, up Strathtay to

Forbin's attempt on Scotland, March 1708. The contemporary grisaille by A. van Salm, National Maritime Museum. The *Dover* has been blocked by *L'Auguste* in her attempt to overtake Forbin in *Le Mars*. The Chevalier de Nangis in *Le Salisbury* is engaged by the *Antelope* and the new British *Salisbury*. The main strength of the English ...

the Castle of Balloch, the seat of the old Earl of Breadalbane. Breadalbane's task would be to keep in check the Argyllshire Campbells, for they would go with their soldier duke. From there Fleming rode south to Castle Drummond to spread the joyous news and have the clanned gentry of Strathearn and beyond make themselves ready for war. On 6th March he was on his way to Stirlingshire to seek out Viscount Kilsyth and to stop at the house nearby of his own brother, the Earl of Wigton, where he learned that Stirlingshire was firm for King James and that the Earl of Linlithgow would take the lead. By 11th March Fleming had ended his mission at the house in Dunbartonshire of Cochrane of Kilmaronock. There Fleming waited for news of the landing; as indeed did all in Scotland who looked back on her valiant history, rather than forward to what glittering prospects union with England might or might not disclose. But it was now getting on to the middle of March, and still there was no word of the ships from France.

All this while, Queen Anne's ministers, and Mr Josiah Burchett, Secretary to the Admiralty in his new office building near Whitehall, had been slow to learn what was afoot at Dunkirk.

The first word had come in early December: their secret agent in Paris reported that 'Count Fourbin' was to command a squadron of ships in the coming year for a purpose unspecified. Later that month he learned that the new squadron would assemble at Dunkirk 'in order to sail to the northward'. In January he reported that it was an attack on some harbour to destroy merchantmen and their escorts as they lay there which was intended.

By now, through the lines of the opposing armies in Flanders reports were coming to the Hague from the spies at Dunkirk that swarms of sailors, companies of marine soldiers and Forbin himself had arrived. That some ship to shore action was in prospect was suggested by the loading of mortar bombs and inflammable 'carcasses' on the ships of the new squadron, the sixty gun *Le Mars*, *Le Jersey* and *L'Auguste*, the two fifty gun prizes from earlier encounters with the English navy, *Le Blackwall* and *Le Salisbury*, and three big forty gun frigates. As they completed their loading each of them moved out to Dunkirk road, the channel of deep water parallel to the shore under the guns of Vauban's fortifications. There was further intelligence that fourteen of the famous Dunkirk privateering frigates, ships of twenty to thirty guns, were to join the squadron.

The first mention that Scotland might be the objective did not come until the middle of February when the projected D-day in the Firth of Forth was only three weeks distant. There had been a report to this effect from Dunkirk, but Dayrolle, the British minister at the Hague said that the Dutch dignitaries there discounted it, holding to the view that an attack on Cadiz to restore the allies' fortunes in Spain – either this or the bombardment of Flushing – was the objective. Even when on 20th February he reported to London that he now had information from France 'of a very good hand' that Scotland was the target, he followed it unhelpfully with speculation that 'the true design . . . could be to transport 8000 men to Corunna to arm the Galicians for an attack on Portugal'. With the army in Flanders Cadogan, Marlborough's deputy while the Captain-General was in London, wondered if it might all be a feint 'to hinder our fleets going into the Mediterranean'.

The moment of truth was near. On the 2nd of March a packet-boat crossed from Holland after a day-long exasperating delay due to the high winds. It informed Queen Anne's ministers that

> The pretended Prince of Wales left Paris on the 8th inst. [O.S. 27th February] to go and embark at Dunkirk for Scotland as it is generally believed in France and published by the Court there.

In Dunkirk, the report continued, there were now thirty-three ships ready to sail including twenty-one fast privateers. Embarkation of the troops now seen to be billeted around Dunkirk could take place in the course of a single night.

The following day Dayrolle informed London that James had arrived in Dunkirk. From Ghent where he was making ready his ten battalions for the crossing to England, Cadogan confirmed this. They would be ready to sail in six days 'if the Zeelanders gave him all the assistance necessary'. (But by then, if everything went to plan, Forbin would be in the Forth.)

Anxiety at the Hague was now somewhat assuaged by a further report from the Dunkirk spies that an English squadron, and a big one, had appeared off Gravelines down the coast from Dunkirk on the same day that James had arrived. Nor could the would-be King embark. One of the spies had been well-placed to see why not:

> On Saturday I was at the King's supper. He had some red spots on his face which he put down to fleas at the inns where he had dined and supped. But when he undressed red spots were found all over his body and he was smitten with fever that night. This was seen to be an attack of measles, and although his own doctor thought he could go on board, those of the town said he could not do so without risking his life.

The later report added that the troops, after going aboard, had now disembarked.

All this was encouraging for Dayrolle and his Dutch friends. Less so was the last piece of intelligence. 'The English fleet disappeared on Sunday'.

If London had been slow to guess Forbin's purpose, this had been on account of the vicious and distracting power-struggle of these wasted months as Harley, the Secretary of State, sought to displace Godolphin, the Lord Treasurer, and curb the power of the Captain-General himself. The drama had reached its climax in early February with the dismissal of Harley by the reluctant, ailing Queen and temporary victory for his enemies. On the heels of this, Dayrolle's report that Scotland could be the objective of French design had come and been placed before the queen on her Sunday evening meeting with her cabinet on 15th February. 'We are a little alarmed', wrote Marlborough to General Lumley in Flanders; but the Captain-General with his customary sang-froid would recognise that an attack on Scotland could at a stroke undo the peaceful Union and cancel the great success already won in six years of war with France. What capital would not enemies nearer home also make of the hideous miscalcula-tions that Scotland would not rise in anger against the contrived Union, that the French would not assist her, and that the navy could keep them away from British shores? A 'protestant wind' had been King James' undoing in 1688: a catholic wind carrying Forbin's squadron to the North might now destroy the queen's ministers twenty years later.

However, the response of the now united administration was vigorous. It was decided there and then that a squadron to watch Dunkirk should be got together at once. Spurred on by Marlborough, the Admiralty, under the effective control of the Admiral his brother, went to work with a will.

All ships on the Thames or Medway or at Portsmouth were to make their way to the Downs; four admirals, Baker, Jennings, Lord Dursley and Sir George Byng were involved in this. Seamen were turned out of ships which were not ready for sea; in the brutal necessity of war, orders went out to impress other seamen from merchantmen. Merchant shipping itself was placed under embargo, and pursers and sailing-masters set to stowing provisions, beer and water. Within a week of the orders being given fifteen sail of the line and nine frigates had assembled in the shelter of the Downs off the Kentish shore. The navy had done well, but the Admiralty still reckoned that it could be Portsmouth which was under threat.

Sir George Byng, recently advanced to Admiral of the Blue, was now next to Sir John Leake, the victor of Malaga (if victory it had been), the most considerable man in the navy. Death, prejudice and intrigue had taken off his rivals. The regularity of Byng's features, the long nose, the oval face, matched the smoothness of his advancement in the service. The problem he now faced in watching Dunkirk was that the great Flemish port could not be sealed, though it seems that this he did not see as clearly as he should. Winds from the north would prevent ships leaving it. Winds from the south would enable a blockading squadron to keep in touch with any ships which emerged. But winds from the east or north-east might enable the enemy to get clear of Dunkirk while driving the blockading force to leeward down the Channel; and if they continued to blow, prevent it weathering the North Foreland or even Dungeness in pursuit. There was also the abiding need to prevent the Brest squadron coming up Channel to join Forbin: it was not only Dunkirk that had to be watched.

Byng anchored his squadron off the Flanders coast on 27th February. Shifting to the 40-gun *Ludlow Castle* he counted for himself the twenty-seven ships now in Dunkirk road; some, he noted, of 50–60 guns. It looked as if the French meant business. That night a Flemish fisherman taken for questioning said that very day his wife had watched the King of England pass their door, thus confirming his worst fears. Byng's instructions were to keep his station off the Flanders coast, but on 1st of March the wind shifted to the westward with signs of dirty weather to come. He had no choice but to take his squadron back to the Downs, though he positioned – if they could hold their station – a small force of frigates and the big 80-gun *Shrewsbury* to the north-east of Dunkirk. At the Downs he found himself still further reinforced, in all twenty-six line-of-battle ships now under his command. He resolved to take the whole force back to Gravelines in a week's time when the tides began to lift: that would be the likeliest time for the French to come out. Learning of this in Whitehall, the Secretary of the Admiralty was apprehensive. What if the French came out before 8th March?

Had Forbin had his way, the French would not have come out at all. To his mind the appearance of English naval strength off the Flanders coast on 27th February was reason enough to cancel the expedition to Scotland. Secrecy had gone: a landing in Scotland would now be impossible. These views he imparted to the unhappy young king, not yet fully recovered from the fever he had apparently caught from his charming sister before he left St Germain. For all his youth and inexperience James would have none of it, even though his elderly advisers, the Duke of Perth and the Earl of Middleton, stood aside. Straightaway a senior officer of the invasion force rode in haste to Versailles with a letter from James to Louis complaining bitterly at Forbin's disembarkation of the expedition's five thousand.

Louis' ministers – some of them – were appalled. The King's dignity was also at risk. Only a week past he had visited St Germain in person to wish young James Godspeed, enjoining him never to give up his religion for the protestant heresy: James had felicitously replied that he hoped it would be long ere he had the honour of seeing him again, and that he would remain in Scotland while even a single castle held out for him – and now it seemed that the invasion fleet would not leave Dunkirk road. Forthwith Louis sent a reply to Dunkirk commanding the angry Forbin to comply with King James' wishes. In the meantime, such had been the tremors from the young king's rage, that Forbin had been forced to send out two advice boats to report on the English fleet. When they returned with the news that it was nowhere to be seen the troops were re-embarked, and James, not yet quite recovered from measles, was huzza'd on board Forbin's flagship, the sixty gun *Le Mars*. To his mother James wrote 'Here I am at last on board. My body is weak but my spirits are high. I hope my next letter will be from the Palace at Edinburgh. I should be there by Saturday.' At Versailles, the court awaited anxiously for the arrival of the daily courier from Dunkirk.

The invasion force set sail from Dunkirk road 'upon the top of the high water with the tide of ebb' in the late afternoon of 6th March; five battleships, two large frigates fitted for transport, twenty-one other frigates. When daylight came they were hidden in the mist, but to deceive scouting English craft the same number of ships were sent out into the road from Dunkirk harbour. First the wind dropped and the squadron had to anchor off Nieuport; then the wind rose with a heavy sea. Held among the shoals off the Flanders coast the squadron was in real danger. Three of the frigates lost their anchors, made signals of distress and drifted away. Aboard *Le Mars* fear was added to sea-sickness. There was nothing to do but ride out the storm all that day and the next. Meanwhile, Versailles, ignorant as yet of the change in the weather, rejoiced that the fleet had sailed at last with excellent prospects of success.

*Le Protée*, was one of the distressed frigates from the great storm of the 7th and the 8th. Most of her forty-four guns had been off-loaded so that she might carry more supplies of war. Her loss to Forbin's squadron would be a serious blow. Recognising this, *lieutenant de frégate* Rambures, her commander, quickly put into Dunkirk to replace the lost anchors. Then he was off to Scotland two days, as he thought, behind his admiral, and shaping a direct course to the Firth of Forth. Three days later, about noon on the 12th, he passed Dunbar and stood into the Firth, making for Leith. Saint-Simon takes up Rambures' story:

As he approached the mouth of the river he saw around him a number of barques and small vessels that he could not avoid . . .

*A New Chart of the Sea Coast of Scotland with the islands thereof. Sold by W. & J. Mount and T. Page on Tower Hill, London.* Early eighteenth century.

The masters of these ships told him that the King was expected with impatience but that they had no news of him, that they had come out to meet him, and that they would send pilots to conduct him up the river to Edinburgh where all was hope and joy.

Rambures went up towards Edinburgh, more and more surrounded by barques which addressed to him the same language. A gentleman of the country passed from one of these barques upon the frigate. [This was James Malcolm of Grange whom Fleming had instructed to meet the French ships when they reached the Forth]. He told Rambures that the principal nobleman of Scotland had resolved to act together, that these noblemen could count upon more than twenty thousand men ready to take up arms and that all the towns only awaited the arrival of the King to proclaim him.

The formal report from *Le Protée* would confirm this. The Scots were indeed ready for the ships from France and vehement that 'at the first signal [of the invasion fleet] all the river would be covered with fishing vessels and others that would readily give their assistance in forwarding the disembarkation'.

In Edinburgh news of the ship from France raised feelings to a new pitch of intensity. When word from London had come the previous week to the Scots Privy Council that an invasion from France was imminent, Jacobite patriotism had burgeoned. Now, Lockhart would recall 'in every person's face was to be observed an air of jollity and satisfaction' excepting government servants (such as the new customs men) and 'such as were deeply dipt in the Revolution'. With these last Lockhart would no doubt number the Commission of the General Assembly of the Church of Scotland. It had on 5th March prayerfully addressed the Almighty in the contorted reasoning of Calvinism: a French invasion was coming, and this was God's 'deserved wrath for these sinful lands'; but prayer might move Him to stay His hand, as it made to skelp poor Scotland, so the first Thursday in April was to be set aside as a solemn day of fasting, humiliation and prayer. But one way or another, all would be over by then.

The more level-headed Earl of Leven, Governor of Edinburgh Castle, also heard of the arrival of *Le Protée* and was sharply aware that there would be no defence against the coming invasion. The mere two thousand of the Scots army could be drawn up on Leith sands, but whether they would fight the Pretender's army was another matter. Nor was the castle in any state to withstand a siege. Leven recognised that flight to Berwick might be the only course for him, but he was not giving up yet. To the Earl of Mar, Secretary of State for Scottish business in London, he reported that the troop of dragoons watching the coast at Dunbar had seized a Jacobite named Hepburn as he sought to go out to the ship from France. Hepburn was one of the stalwarts who had held the Bass Rock for James VII fifteen years ago, but to Leven he was 'an ingrained rogue' who would confess nothing. 'I have caged him in the Castle of Edinburgh', he added.

On *Le Protée* as night came on and still there was no sign of his admiral, Rambures' anxiety deepended. At first light he took his ship down the Firth on the ebb to look for Forbin. In the jaws of the Firth, from Fife Ness to the Bass Rock he saw a forest of sail. As he came nearer he could make out *Le Mars* and the other ships of the line in Forbin's squadron bearing down on a squadron of English ships, four times his number.

Forbin too had recognised how serious a loss to the expedition would be the drifting away of *Le Protée* and the other distressed frigates in the great storm. They carried a sixth of the soldiery and more than that proportion of munitions. Here was another pretext to call off the attempt on Scotland. As the storm abated off the Flanders coast a council of war was held in King James' apartment on *Le Mars* to consider whether the voyage should be continued. With Forbin was the Comte de Gacé (now with his marshal's brevet and to be known as the Maréchal de Matignon). Again the young king showed firmness of purpose in the face of French diffidence: the attempt on Scotland must be made. Forbin was asked to send word to Dunkirk that the three ships should make their way to Scotland with all haste.

That settled, the council of war on *Le Mars* set to deliberating where in Scotland to make the landing. Hooke, since ten days past a Brigadier and Lord Hooke in the Jacobite peerage, was the principal adviser. He now proposed a landing at Montrose, with the certainty of support from the Angus nobility and gentry. Lord Middleton, seemingly out of character, was for a bolder course. Forbin, he said, should run his squadron up the Firth of Forth and disembark at Burntisland which lay on its north side, opposite to Leith. From there the invading five thousand could move quickly on Stirling, the key to Scotland. Edinburgh too was within easy range. With the crown jewels of Scotland (and the Equivalent) recovered from their incarceration in the castle, young James could be crowned King of Scots. Middleton's views prevailed; but perhaps Hooke had had a premonition that in the event, Forbin would not hazard his ships by sailing them up the Firth in the way he must.

Then they were off to the north in a brisk gale of following wind. Some further hours had been lost in lying-to so that the squadron might reassemble after the great storm, but still more of the precious advantage of time was sacrificed by the course which Forbin now shaped. His rage at having been commanded by Louis to conform to the young king's wishes was unabated; many years later, in compiling his memoirs the resentment he still felt at this glowed, irrationally and unpleasantly, as he recalled how he had jeered at his passengers' distress as *La Mars* pitched and rolled in the heavy sea. Now it was his distaste for the whole enterprise that was in command. As the journal of the pilot François Gavarry records, the squadron sailed on a course north-west by north which on the 10th March took it to a landfall on the Yorkshire coast, five leagues off Robin Hood's Bay. There was every prospect of arrival off the Firth of Forth on the morning of 11th. But now there occurred a strange diversion out to sea. 'Under press of sail all night', recorded Gavarry 'and this morning [12th March] saw the coast of Aberdeen west north-west, twelve leagues distant'. The mystery is the greater in that Gavarry's journal – or rather the copy of it he made for Hooke at the latter's request – seems to omit the 11th March altogether, and from then is a day out of step.

On the morning of the 12th, Hooke, unable to sleep, was on the deck of *Le Mars* as she approached Scotland. To his horror he now saw emerge from the darkness not the welcoming brazier-light on the Isle of May but the sweep of the Aberdeenshire coast, all of a hundred miles north of the Forth, which he had come to know from his two previous voyages to Slains. Was it simple confusion over the squadron's dead reckoning? Was it, he wondered, treachery?

The faulty landfall recognised, Forbin's ships turned south. With the wind gone round to the north-east it might yet be possible to reach the Forth before the English navy. The townsfolk of Stonehaven saw the squadron on its southward track. Some fisherman who went out to a 32-gun frigate which came inshore were spoken to in Scots by 'some gentlemen in scarlet'; their wondering eyes also noticed the ship's 'blackamoor servants'. As his ships came southward Forbin sent a frigate ahead. Rounding Fife Ness she put in close to the fishing burgh of Pittenweem and took on board a pilot for the passage up Firth. By evening on the 12th the whole squadron was passing between the low shore-line of Fife Ness and May Island. Instead of pressing on, he brought his ships to anchor in Crail Road and resolved to wait there till morning. A Crail boat went out to *Le Mars*; as the admiral's ship she flew the white flag of France at her topmast. Some of her people shouted that they intended to land, that they were worried over the whereabouts of the English fleet, that they had aboard 'the prisoner' whom Scotland awaited; and they plied the Fifers with drink.

On the day on which Forbin sailed from Dunkirk, Byng's ships had put to sea to resume the watch on Dunkirk, but the wind dropped and they had to anchor in mid-Channel between Dover and Calais. The great seas which kept Forbin perilously at anchor off the Flanders coast on Sunday 7th March and Monday 8th now drove Byng down Channel to shelter from the easterlies in Rye Bay, behind Dungeness. Sir George was not troubled that he had temporarily to give up his watch on the French ships. So long as the wind blew from the east, he reckoned complacently that it 'locks them fast in Dunkirk from going to Scotland'.

As the storm blew itself out on the 8th Byng sailed for Dunkirk, just at the time Forbin went off to the north. As he took up station off Dunkirk road on the 9th Byng had word from Cadogan at Ostend: the night before there had been twenty-seven ships off Nieuport preparing to sail, and in the morning they had gone. With naval taciturnity he foreborne to express his feelings about this to the Admiralty, informing their Lordships simply that he was leaving Rear-Admiral Baker to convoy the British regiments which must now be hastened over to England, and that he himself was off in pursuit of the French who had gone 'as we imagine to the Forth'. Meanwhile at Westminster, as the news spread of Forbin's escape from Dunkirk, Parliament was in a hubbub with the coming invasion; and in the City there was a run on the Bank of England (engineered, it seems, by the Bank's commercial rivals but an indication of panic nonetheless). There was also talk of treachery at the highest level: that it had all been Harley's doing.

Though he now greatly outnumbered the French, Sir George was well aware that his heavy ships could not match the speed through the water of the Dunkirk privateers, and that some of his squadron were the slower for being foul and in need of cleaning. This should give the French a crucial further day's advantage. All he could do was to shape the direct course to the Forth which with the wind favouring it was now in his power to do. By noon on Friday 12th March the Cheviot hills were in sight. Around midnight he and his squadron anchored some miles to the east of the May, and the *Lark* advice-boat was sent to the island's flaming light-house for news of the Frenchmen: had they gone up the Firth? When first light came six hours later Byng had his answer: there, a dozen miles to the north-west was Forbin's squadron in Crail road. It was now open to the English admiral to entrap his French adversary in the Firth.

On *Le Mars* as the sky lightened in the east revealing the English squadron, had her passengers in the general consternation and dismay had time for reflection they must have bitterly regretted the waste of previous day's opportunity. Now the tide was ebbing back to the open sea and the wind was going round to the north-west. It was too late. Yet, had Forbin recognised (or had explained to him?) the expedition's crucial importance for France, by now his flagship, her

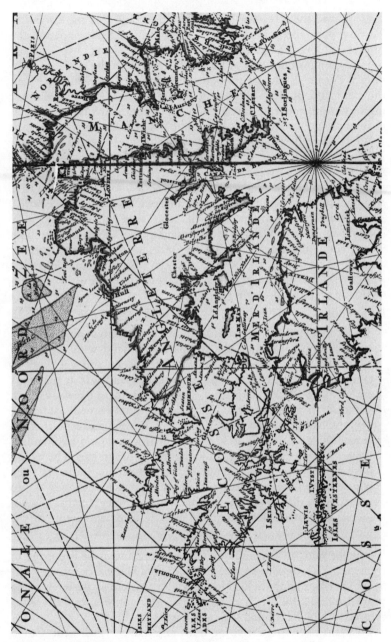

From the *Carte de la Mer d'Allemagne* in *Le Neptune François ou Atlas Nouveau des Cartes Marines*, Paris 1695. This was the naval atlas commissioned for his navy by Louis XIV.

consorts and the privateers would have been well into the disembarkation of men and munitions on to the swarming fishing boats of the Fife coast. The change in the wind would have tended to lock the pursuing Englishmen out of the Firth. Even with the evident weakness of Forbin's strategic grasp, had the Duke of Berwick rather than the mild and polite Maréchal de Matignon been the expedition's military commander, the invasion of Scotland would now have begun at Burntisland, in full view of the ramparts of Edinburgh castle.

While Versailles had waited for word that Forbin had sailed from Dunkirk with his troops and royal passenger, Berwick newly arrived from Spain, had been received by Louis. Saint-Simon noted that the king had kept him waiting – and this was not his wont – and that after an audience of half an hour Berwick came out 'tout rouge et echauffé'. That Louis' youngest marshal who was also James' half-brother should have been so red and ruffled suggests that there had been high words about the elderly Comte de Gacé having been preferred as military commander. To the end of his days Berwick was clear what should have happened when Forbin reached the Forth. To any objection that Forbin might have lost all his Dunkirkers in another La Hogue along the sands of Burntisland, Berwick was adamant:

> This consideration ought not to have prevented him; for the material point was, that the troops should land with the young King: all Scotland expected him with impatience, and was ready to take arms in his favour: what is more, England was at that time entirely unprovided with troops, so that he might have advanced, without resistance, into the North, where numbers of considerable persons had promised to join them. It is even probable that his sister, Queen Anne, apprehending a civil war, would have endeavoured to come to some terms with him, by which means he would have been sure of ascending the throne of his ancestors. The consternation was so great at London, that the bank was like to break, every man hastening to withdraw his money: but the news of the ill success of the enterprise soon restored the credit of the Government.

It was, he said, all Chamillart's doing, intriguing as he had done to transform his crony the Comte de Gacé into a Marshal of France. 'The Scots', Berwick added in his Memoirs with a bitterness the intervening years had not dulled, 'had asked earnestly for me, but the King refused, saying he wanted me elsewhere.'

Lockhart likewise gave voice to his rage and bewilderment. Could not the ships from France, he asked, have sailed past Edinburgh to the windings of the Forth where the English ships could not follow? The strangest irony was that as he lay at anchor off Crail, Forbin had fired signal guns and shown lights to attract a response from the shore which came only in the form of the boat-load of Fifers looking for a drink. But under James Malcolm of Grange there had been a reception committee: earlier that day it had sailed up the Forth with *Le Protée*.

Today with an eye to the strategic prize within France's grasp one can only echo the words of the Duke of Berwick and George Lockhart of Carnwath. There might have been spectactular feats for many young Hornblowers of the Royal Navy to perform in cutting out work on Burntisland sands or somewhere between Queensferry and the upper reaches of the Forth. But the purposes of France would have been served. Scotland would have been set ablaze.

To return to the daylight off May Island on 13th March. The presence of a vastly superior English fleet apparently locking him into the Firth was the kind of challenge to which Forbin was equal. At once he sent off *L'Americaine* to look more closely at the English men-of-war; then with the wind backing to the north-west he boldly stood to the southwards towards Byng as if the Dunkirkers would board his great ships. Seeing the Frenchmen coming down on him Byng formed his ships into a line of battle and lay to, not attempting to split his force as he might well have done to close the exit from the Firth between Fife Ness and May Island. Having thus made Byng conform to his wishes, Forbin turned towards the open sea and with the wind on the port beam with his swifter ships steered for the north-east. It was a neat escape.

In Byng's squadron the 54-gun *Dover* was clean, as was the 40-gun *Ludlow Castle*. As Forbin's ships made off, they overtook *Le Salisbury* which had the rearguard, under command of the Chevalier de Nangis, Forbin's senior captain. Standing athwart, *L'Auguste* came to her aid, as did *Le Griffon*. From mid-afternoon until nightfall the French and English ships cannonaded each other off the Angus coast, while *Le Mars* and the rest of the French squadron to signals from their admiral stood to the north and escaped. By now the British *Salisbury*, the *Antelope* and the *Leopard*, each 54-gun ships were coming into the action, and the wind was dropping.

By the early hours of Sunday the 14th *Le Salisbury* was alone and ringed with enemies. The British *Salisbury* drifted on board and de Nangis struck his colours. The five years his ship had spent in the service of the King of France were over. As the two ships ground together in the darkness the *Leopard* – not the *Dover* or the *Ludlow Castle* which had taken the brunt of the fighting – got a boat away and made *Le Salisbury* her prize. We have already met the captain of the *Leopard*: he was Thomas Gordon, formerly master of the *Royal Mary*, the frigate of the Scots navy which had kept out of the way of Colonel Hooke on his voyages to Slains!

As he made off to the north with the rest of the squadron Forbin now let slip his third opportunity. The young King, who, unlike the others, had earned Forbin's admiration for having shewn no fear during the storm that beset the squadron off the Flanders' coast, demanded that he be set on shore even if it were only with his Scotsmen and Matignon. It does seem from the lengthy passage in his Memoirs that Forbin was unable to understand the purpose of the young king's request. He ascribed it wrongly to James' fear, as he watched the plight of the rearguard far astern, that the English ships would overtake them all. Forbin rightly insisted that this would not happen. But it seems that what James sought unsuccessfully to slip past the admiral's obstinacy was recognition that Scotland would rise for him even if he were the only one to land; and that with Jacobite Angus now on the port beam there was nothing to fear for his safety were he put ashore. In his wilful ignorance that this was so, Forbin now refused to comply with young James' demand; nor did the good-natured army commander seek to exercise his new authority as a Marshal of France to make him do so. Had the Duke of Berwick held the command he would have overborne the choleric admiral.

Rather than land James on the Angus shore, or at the Earl Marischal's Dunottar, Forbin now proposed that the squadron should round Buchan Ness, enter the Moray Firth and land passengers, troops and supplies at Inverness or in the shelter of the Cromarty Firth. This caused James to drop his demand that he be put ashore *instanter*. They were now about the level of Aberdeen and getting out of sight of the English fleet: it might after all be better that he and his expedition keep together. *L'Americaine* was sent ahead with James Ogilvie to seek pilots from the fishermen of Portsoy, close to the now deserted castle of Boyne which had been his home. However, on Monday the 15th a stubborn wind got up from the west and shewed no sign of abating. While it blew the Moray Firth was closed to Forbin.

Here, at last, young James' spirit cracked. At a council of war the admiral emphasised the dangers to the squadron were they to continue to tack to and fro under the lee of the Aberdeenshire coast. In fact there was no danger from Byng: rightly cautious, he was taking his ships back to the Forth lest Forbin should attempt to double round him. Forbin also spoke of the want of provisions, for much had been thrown overboard to lighten ship in the flight to the north. The Duke of Perth had no judgement to offer, and all along the Earl of Middleton had probably felt that military adventure was no way to secure a Stuart succession. Yet, all along the Moray Firth, as Hooke could attest, Jacobite feeling was high; and these March westerlies could change. James might have insisted on going on, as his eldest son would do when *he* came to the Highlands of Scotland thirty-seven years later. Now the decision was taken to return to Dunkirk. The fault was not in the young king's stars but in himself, as Saint-Simon recognised.

He showed much will and firmness which he spoiled by a docility the result of a bad education, austere and confined which a confused sort of devotion, together with the desire of maintaining him in fear and dependence, caused the Queen to give him.

James had done well, but not well enough. He was still mother-ridden, and this was his undoing.

A great storm from the east now tossed the French squadron. The same winds that blew the *Dover* and *Ludlow Castle* all the way from Buchan Ness to Foula drove *Le Blackwall* and the smaller *L'Ecureuil* far into the Atlantic. For *Le Mars* and the rest of the squadron return to Dunkirk was disorderly and took nearly two weeks. It is unlikely that there was any gladness of heart at the King's table as he dined in company with fifty other guests at Forbin's expense each day. It was a well appointed table, Forbin recalled in his Memoirs as if this somehow offset the calamity; the broth made in great cauldrons each morning, pheasant or other game everyday and a multitude of cooks for the ragouts and deserts. How below deck the long suffering rank and file of the French regiments fared he did not mention. Their habitual good spirits, sustained by regimental song and addiction to tobacco must have been sorely tested; not all would survive the ordeal. But return to Dunkirk was safely achieved. The Admiralty had hastily assembled a squadron from ships which had not been made ready in time to join Sir George Byng and positioned it off Dunkirk – or would have done so had Griffiths its commander been able to find enough pilots. As it was, only half this scratch squadron stood in Forbin's way as he made back to the Flanders coast. Twenty miles off Dunkirk they saw him on 25th of March. Captain Griffiths should have recognised that strengths were about equal and that the crowded Frenchmen were in poor condition for a fight. But he forebore to attack.

On 28th March at Dunkirk Thomas Quicke and Edward and John Turner, 'mariners lately belonging to the Hooker gally of London' which had earlier been taken by a Dunkirk privateer, saw James come ashore from *Le Mars* 'a tall, slight young man with a pale smooth face, a blue feather in his hat and a star on his cloak'. They observed that while he had been huzza'd as he went on board at the beginning of the month he now came ashore in silence. Forbin had failed him. At some point in the voyage Perth and Middleton, with Scottish passion for genealogy had informed the admiral that he was descended from an

Aberdeenshire Forbes who had gone abroad to be a soldier in the 13th century. It would have been fitting had Forbin been the instrument of James' restoration but it was not to be.

'On board the *Medway* before Leith, the 22nd of March 1707/08 at nine at night', Sir George Byng wrote to Rear-Admiral Baker, already off Tynemouth Bar with the regiments which Cadogan had despatched from Ostend. His clerk writing by candle-light, and he dictating with an economy of words, Sir George said,

> I can give you no further account of the enemy than that on the 13th we found their squadron at an anchor off the Firth of Edinburgh, they got under saile, stood out to sea, we chased them as farr as Buchaness, took out the *Salisbury*, the rest got away in the night, the next morning we saw nineteen of them as farr as we could see from the mast-head to the eastward of us. That day being little wind and no hopes of further chasing them, we lay off and on to geather our ships together and repair the damage the *Dover* and the *Salisbury* had in their scuffle, and another ship of ours that received damage in her masts.

He continued,

> On this day sevenight the wind blowing hard north easterly we bore up for this place, have not heard any manner of account of them since, though we have had four scouts out, two of which lay off Aberdeen and other two off Buchaness. The two that were off Aberdeen came into us this morning, haveing not seen a saile in the sea . . .

Sir George concluded by saying that he had 'sent an express to Court' for orders. If Prince George [Prince George of Denmark, Queen Anne's husband, in charge at the Admiralty] agreed he would forthwith sail for the Downs 'and if the weather permit will look into Flemish Road on the way thither'. He ended with a brotherly message of good wishes to Baker from his colleagues, Jennings and Lord Dursley.

Prudently, the Admiralty required Byng to remain on the coast of Scotland a while longer. Five days later Byng again wrote to Baker, this time in his own hand:

> I am getting under sail and intend to stand to and fro off of Buchaness for eight and fortie houers, then I shall return to this place againe if I hear no more of the enemy . . . If I learn any account of the enemy I will dispatch away an express to you. If I hear nothing more of them I shall conclude they are gone home.

But March in the Firth of Forth had taken its toll. 'I am almost dead with a cold', Sir George concluded, 'my head readie to split'.

Last of all a thought should be spared for the British infantry Rear-Admiral Baker had escorted from Ostend to the Tyne. In his manuscript 'Journal of the Campaign in Flanders A.D. MDCCVIII', Private Deane of the First Battalion of Foot Guards narrates how orders had come on 8th March to the ten regiments of foot at Ghent. There they embarked in vessels and were towed by horses to Bruges. On the 15th they marched to Ostend and shipped on board the *Bonadventure*, setting sail on the 17th. 'On March 21st about 1 o'clock in the afternoon we came to anchor att Tinmouth where we lay for further orders, labouring under many inconveniences, haveing only the bare deck to lye upon which hardship caused abundance of our men to bid adieu to the world'. Riding out rough weather off Tynemouth Bar, their ordeal was not yet over. On 1st April the *Bonadventure* sailed for Leith where Byng's fleet still lay. There Deane's company was transhipped to the *Dreadnought* man-of-war and conveyed back to the Tyne and to transports which, in consistently foul weather, sailed over to Flanders with the ten regiments, including the one which would come to be known as the Royal Scots, and another already known as the Scots Fusiliers. Not until 21st April did they disembark at Ostend.

Words did not fail Private Deane in depicting the purgatory on board,

While we lay on board we had continual distruction in the foretop, the Pox above board, the plague between decks, hell in the forecastle, and the Devil at the helm.

All this and a crooked purser who 'was dayly blest with the souldier's prayers'.

# 3

# The Cover-Up

*Thus failed a project so well and so secretly conducted until the end. It was lamentable. And with this project failed that of the Low Countries which was no longer thought of.*

Such was Saint-Simon's verdict on *L'entreprise d'Ecosse*. An operation of war, imaginatively planned, and though too long delayed blessed at last with a favourable wind, one which was directed towards a Scotland largely united against England and with virtually no countervailing force of arms from the proponents of Union, all this had been made to seem no more than a gambler's throw. It was indeed lamentable. Now came the cover-up.

First back to Dunkirk was the 24-gun *Le Zéphyr* and her eight companies of the Boulonnais, just five days after Forbin's encounter with Byng off the Firth of Forth. Her captain claimed that his ship had proved to be a bad sailer and had been unable to keep up with the rest of the squadron as it ran to the north. In the distance he had watched an English man-of-war (this would be the 54-gun *Dover*) mingle with the squadron's rearguard, open fire with her great guns and with rockets, and signal to other ships ahead of the main English fleet to join in the fight. Discretion being the better part of valour he had 'judged it proper to return to Dunkirk as the wind was favourable'. He also said that he was fearful about the rest of the squadron. It was to be hoped that they had been able to disperse: that might have been their only hope of survival.

The army being eager to find out where the navy had gone wrong, a M. de Bernières, one of Chamillart's officials at Dunkirk, set to questioning the pilots of *Le Zéphyr* about the failure to effect a landing on the Scottish coast before the English fleet came up. They claimed that on the run to the north there had been 'a fresh and hard gale which obliged them to stand out to sea', but they made no mention of the disastrously wrong landfall; and in recognising that the English fleet had made such good time to Scotland apparently by shaping a direct course to the Forth they did not touch on the point that their own admiral might have done likewise. As to the meeting with the English fleet, 'the inequality of forces being considered', they said, 'M. Forbin pursued the only course he could take which was to put to sea with a pressing sail towards the north of Scotland, and to escape from the enemy during the night'. It was still hoped, added Bernières, that the young king and the troops would have been able to land 'at Cromarty which is a port in the north of Scotland'.

Next day *Le Protée* came back. Her commander had not the same need to make excuses. He described his triumphal arrival in the Forth on the morning of Friday, 12th March, his view the following morning of the arrival of the English fleet and of Forbin's flight to the north. He had, he said, done what he could to draw some of the Englishmen away from his admiral, and then he had returned to Dunkirk.

There followed two weeks or more of foreboding at Dunkirk, at Versailles, and at the Palace of St Germain, and then on 6th April after three weeks at sea part of Forbin's squadron returned. Their admiral, they said, was not far away; off the Texel bad weather had separated them a few days past. Their pilots admitted to Bernières that there had been a faulty landfall on the Scottish coast, but by how much they did not say. They gave the dismal news that the projected landing on the sheltered shores of the Cromarty Firth had not taken place; they said (erroneously) that *L'Americaine*, sent ahead to look for pilots, had been unable to find any; and they claimed (falsely) that off the Moray Firth 'the enemy's fleet forthwith appearing chased ours so briskly that they were obliged to lay aside their design of attempting a descent'.

The following day when the Admiral's flagship, *Le Mars*, returned to Dunkirk road, D'Andrezel who had been a passenger on board sent his report of the fiasco to Chamillart. He said that even if the landing had taken place, the success of the expedition would have been doubtful; and with the Gallic aptitude for making defeat seem like success he added that, '. . . it was very fortunate to have brought back to Dunkirk the King of England, the ships, the troops, and the money, after running so great a risk'. Nor would Matignon rock the boat. Writing to the king, as was his privilege as a Marshal of France, he merely expressed his mortification at the expedition's ill-success. His only criticism of Forbin was that the admiral had not been courteous enough to give him the opportunity of reporting to the king by the same courier who took a dispatch from the squadron to Pontchartrain, Minister of the Navy at Paris. (The 'courier' whom the King's new marshal did not deign to name was, apparently, Brigadier Hooke).

If from his Memoirs of so many years later we may guess how Forbin now explained himself to Pontchartrain he too would be evasive. The faulty landfall would be put at a mere half-dozen leagues – less than twenty miles – to the north of the Forth, whereas the Aberdeenshire coast which Hooke discerned with such dismay in the early hours of

12th March lay a full hundred miles north; and Saint-Simon for his part sensed a cover-up to ineptitude. 'The Comte de Forbin', he remarked with some acidity, 'had twice got out of his reckoning within forty eight hours, a fact not easy to understand on a voyage from Ostend to Edinburgh.' Much would also be made of the tides in the Forth and the seeming lack of response to Forbin's signals from the Fife shore. Gavarry's journal states that the wind was not strong enough to enable the squadron to sail over the tide on the evening of the 12th, but perhaps it could have pressed on up the Forth when the tide changed a few hours later with the wind still from the north.

Hooke was bitter, although Louis was to reward him handsomely. A note in the hand of the younger Nathaniel's cousin at the end of the papers now in the Bodleian records – the words underlined – that the papers impounded by the French court in 1740 were strongly critical of Forbin's conduct as admiral. (It was Forbin rather than the pilot he seems to have blamed: among those papers about the events of 1708 which were impounded by the Court and survived is a letter from the pilot, M Gavarry, seeking help to secure payment for his services). Nathaniel Hooke also recorded that his uncle was asked by St Germain to undertake yet another mission to Scotland later in 1708, and declined. But still the assiduous official, he was deep in planning the following year at Versailles for a descent on Scotland from Brest, such as the Duke of Berwick had proposed. At last Louis had recognised the value of the Scottish card but by now with the British navy so much in the ascendant it was too late: planning was abandoned and the war ground on ruinously for France with further defeat in Flanders. Lord Hooke went on to a substantial diplomatic career in the service of France and enrolment as a Knight in the Order of St Louis: but the 'Scotch business', as he termed it, was not revived.

There was no flicker of admission that failure was due to French shortcomings when James and his mother visited Louis at Marly in the mid-April of 1708. The story that before young James had left St Germain in late February Louis had given him the royal appurtenances of a sword, its hilt set in diamonds, a royal wardrobe, rich liveries, splendid uniforms and services of gold and silver plate is probably apocryphal, but even so the April meeting could not but be distressing. 'The visit was altogether a sad one', noted Saint-Simon. 'The Courts which met in the garden returned towards the château

*Facing*, The governmental response in the House of Commons on 8th March 1709 to criticism of its unreadiness for the attempt on Scotland. Pages 247 and 248 of *A Collection of the Parliamentary Debates in England from the year MDCLXVIII* Vol. V. Printed in 1741.

A. 1709. DEBATES. 247

Lordſhips, that after the *invaſion* was over, there were *eſtimates* made, what it would *coſt to put the fortifications of* Scotland *in good repair.* The total, as appears by your ſchedule, amounts to 23156 *l.* of which there could be but 3000 *l.* laid out this year ; and yet there has been but poor 1500 *l.* expended upon that ſervice this year, as appears by your paper.

I will not trouble you farther, I think this matter is now very plain before your Lordſhips ; I could wiſh I had not ſaid one word of truth in what I have ſaid to you ; but the vouchers ſhew it to be ſo, and if all this be true, it is *a very ſtrange, a very ſurprizing, and a very aſtoniſhing truth.*

I ſhall not move any thing to your Lordſhips farther in this matter, I believe there has been enough now ſaid, to juſtify thoſe Lords for moving this enquiry, and ſhall add but this word, that if there be no greater care taken for the future, than there was at this time of ſuch imminent danger, *it will be the greateſt miracle in the world, if without a miracle the* Pretender *be not placed upon that throne.*

This is the ſubſtance of what was obſerved by the Lord *Haverſham*, tho' there happened ſome *interlocutories* between him and another Lord : And the obſervations were made upon the papers as they were read : The Duke of *Buckingham* and ſeveral others ſpoke to the ſame effect : Upon which it was ordered, that that important affair ſhould be conſidered the *Tueſday* following in a full houſe.

On the 8th of *March* the Commons took into conſideration the papers relating to the deſigned *invaſion* of *Scotland*, and the proceedings thereupon, and againſt the Lord *Griffin* and others taken in rebellion ; and relating to the perſons taken upon ſuſpicion, as alſo to the garriſons of *Scotland.* Whereupon the houſe *reſolved, Firſt,* ' That orders were

*Votes of the Commons, approving the conduct of the government about the invaſion.*

R 4 ' not

' not iffued for the marching of the troops in *Eng-*
' *land* until the 14th day of *March*, it being neceffa-
' ry for the fecurity of her Majefty's perfon and
' government, that the troops in this part of the
' kingdom fhould not march into *Scotland*, till there
' was certain intelligence that the enemy intended
' to land in that part of the united Kingdom. *Se-*
' *condly*, That timely and effectual care was taken
' by thofe employed under her Majefty, at the time
' of the intended invafion of *Scotland*, to difappoint
' the defigns of her Majefty's enemies both at home
' and abroad, by fitting out a fufficient number of
' men of war, ordering a competent number of
' troops from *Flanders*, giving directions for the
' forces in *Ireland* to be ready for the affiftance of
' the nation, and by making the neceffary and pro-
' per difpofitions of the forces in *England*.'

The houfe of Lords on the 28th of *April*, fent down
a bill to the Commons, which their Lordfhips had
paffed ; it was intituled, *An act for improving the
Union of the two kingdoms*, to which they defired the
others concurrence. The bill being read twice, was
referred to a Committee of the whole houfe ; and
on the 5th of this month, they ordered that the
faid Committee fhould be impowered to receive one
or more claufe or claufes, for afcertaining what
offences fhould be adjudged high-treafon, or mif-
prifion of treafon ; the method of profecution and
trial ; and the forfeitures and punifhments for fuch
forts of offences throughout the united kingdom of *Great-Britain*, in fuch manner as might be
more conducive to the fecurity of her Majefty's
perfon and government, the fucceffion as by law
eftablifhed in the proteftant line, and for the attaint-
ing of the Pretender: Then the Commons in a
grand Committee took the faid bill into confidera-
tion, which occafioned a warm debate ; the *Scotch*
members making feveral fpeeches againft the claufe,
for rendering the *Scots*, in cafes of treafon, liable
to

exchanging small talk in a small way'. However, he noted that Louis gave Middleton a long and withering look, and the gossip was that he was suspected of having betrayed the attempt on Scotland to the government in London. The official line was that which Voltaire reproduced nearly half a century later in his *Le Siecle de Louis* XIV: it had contributed to the glory of France that the Scottish project should even have been attempted.

As to the miscarrying of the attempt Voltaire, informed one imagines by the aged Torcy, but in ignorance of the strictures which Saint-Simon said were privately made of Forbin's conduct, went on to produce a string of excuses. The ministry in London had anticipated the attempt, he said, and had recalled beforehand the battalions from Flanders (which was not so); simultaneously, they had arrested the ringleaders in Edinburgh (which was equally untrue); and the Scots had failed to answer Forbin's signals.

Forbin, however, had no further employment. The king recompensed him with two thousand écus for his expense in entertaining his passengers and awarded him a pension of a thousand; but the chef d'escadre did not attain the coveted rank of lieutenant-general, so he retired to a complacent old age in Provence. There he wrote in completion of his dubious Memoirs 'I . . . breathe a very good air and lead a very comfortable quiet life, entirely devoted to the service of my Creator and the cultivation of my friends'. But the last word was with Saint-Simon, acidly critical of Portchartrain's malign delaying influence as he was of Forbin. In bringing the invasion attempt to nothing the latter, he said, had in his own way served the purpose of the Navy Minister well indeed.

In England, relief at the failure of the French invasion was followed by anger that Louis should ever have attempted it. At Versailles, Saint-Simon was acutely aware how counter-productive to French interests it had all been on the other side of the Channel and in Holland.

The allies uttered loud cries against this attempt by a power which they believed to be at its last gasp, and which while pretending to seek peace thought of nothing less than the ruin of Great Britain. The effect of our failure was to bind closer, and irritate more and more their formidable alliance.

This greatly helped the Whig interest at the elections in May 1708 for what would be the first Parliament of Great Britain. Their influence on government was now dominant, though the prestige of the queen's ministers rose again in July with Marlborough's second great victory in Flanders, the overwhelming of Vendôme's army near the fortress-town of Oudenarde.

However, the High Tory peer, Lord Haversham, ever a tiresome critic of government, still saw in the tardy response there had been to 'the alarm from Dunkirk' of February and March a stick with which to beat Godolphin. January of 1709 found him in the House of Lords demanding an official enquiry. When had government first learned of the intended invasion of Scotland? 'What orders were thereupon issued into Scotland with relation either to forces or garrisons? What was the number of regular troops and forces there at the time of the intelligence? What was the state of the garrisons there at the time? What augmentation was made, or forces sent thither from the time of the intelligence?'

Marlborough and Godolphin, whose minds in that winter of 1707–8 had been on Flanders, or taken up with the bitter fight to maintain their position against the queen's favouring of Secretary of State Harley, had indeed too blithely assumed that in the aftermath of Union Scotland would remain quiet. Both now seemed vulnerable.

As demanded by Haversham, an inquiry was instituted by the House of Lords, and the outcome was the pile of state papers before the House on 25th February 1709. Here was the wide variety of intelligence coming across the Channel and from Flanders in the winter months about the build-up of naval and military strength at Dunkirk. Here were the letters that flew between Sir George Byng and the Secretary at the Admiralty in the anxious days of late February and March. Lord Haversham wished particularly to expose the correspondence from the Earl of Leven, lieutenant-general and commander-in-chief in Scotland, to the queen's ministers in London. On the day Forbin dropped anchor off Crail Leven had written from Edinburgh castle.

Here I am, not one farthing of money to provide provision or for contingencies or intelligence; none of the commissions yet sent down; few troops and those almost naked. It vexes me sadly to think I must retire towards Berwick if the French land on this side the Forth.

Haversham's attempt to drum up fears that the French might come again, and his thinly-veiled allegation that the want of preparation argued treachery among the queen's ministers, gained no support. When the debate was resumed in the Lords on 1st March 1709 the House was content to ask for assurances that Scotland had by now been sufficiently strengthened. As to the Commons, they simply endorsed the government's disingenuous response that orders had not been given to move troops to Scotland until the day after the French appeared in the Forth because it could not be foreseen where the enemy was to strike; and (with some effrontery) that the government's naval and military dispositions had been 'timely and effectual'.

There it rested. As governments have found down the years, nothing conceals like success. Daniel Defoe recognised what a close-run thing it had been: only 'the immediate interposition of a Divine Power' had saved the day. But, government propagandist that he was, he forbore to criticise the queen's ministers in his *History of the Union of Great Britain* published that year.

In the debate in the House of Commons there was some criticism – not pressed home – of Sir George Byng for having failed to trap Forbin's squadron in the jaws of the Firth of Forth. Admirals being political as well as professional appointments in those days, party feeling may well have inspired the criticism. In his report of the action Sir George had indeed glossed over his failure to divide his great preponderance of strength so as to entrap the enemy whichever way they steered out of the Firth. (Sir George's tragic son would display the same excessive caution off Minorca in 1756). A Rodney or a Nelson would not have let Forbin off so lightly.

The cover-up in Scotland was just as complete. At the laird of Kilmaronock's house near Glasgow, Charles Fleming had waited impatiently in the March days of 1708 for news that the king had landed. When he heard that James had landed somewhere 'benorth of Tay' he set out on a circuitous route through Perthshire, catching up on the way with a party of Stirlingshire lairds, armed as were their men, and, like him, still hopeful. But already Edinburgh Jacobites were chilled by the spectacle of Byng's tall ships casting anchor off Leith. While word circulated that there had been no landing, throughout the north, as the Earl of Leven said, gentlemen were 'upon the wing'.

Leven was still in great anxiety. Until they had been recognised for what they were the appearance of Sir George's ships caused him to draw up his meagre army on Leith Sands in such battle array as it could muster. For the next two weeks, only too well aware that with the British fleet back in the Forth there was nothing to interrupt a landing further north, Leven remained a worried man. This anxiety lessened only slowly. He had conflicting reports that French ships were in the Cromarty Firth or that they had been seen near Mull and might fall on Fort William at the southern end of the Great Glen. 'I must own that it passes my reach to make any conjecture what can become of the French fleet with the Pretender', he wrote to Mar, his Secretary of State in London. 'It is now a full fortnight since they saw any enemy to oppose them, and yet that there should be no account of their landing is very surprising. That they are still not far from the coast is more than probable. Nothing can be plainer to me that they daily lose and we daily gain by their delay in landing'. Kindly as he was clear-sighted, Leven spared a thought for the enemy, reflecting on 'how much both soldiers and seamen must suffer by being so long on board when so extremely crowded'.

There was however firm word that there had been two ships in the Moray Firth 'close by the land before Cullen' on the 17th. (One of these would be L'Americaine). An officer had come on shore 'and caused carry claret wine with him and went to Buckie where he was attended by a great many gentlemen who lived thereabout and drunk there a pretty while very heartily'. The following day, 18th March, another ship joined them and all three thereupon took in fresh water at Speymouth. The report continued:

They have diverted themselves on shore all this day at gaming and own themselves publicly to be French which has caused great preparations to be made by all the gentlemen in the Enzie.

The 17th of March was only four days after Forbin's run from the Forth. The westerlies which kept him out of the Moray Firth had soon died. Could it as easily have been King James who now came ashore to the enthusiastic welcome from Gordon of Buckie and other Gordon and Innes gentry, and perhaps the Duke of Gordon himself?

It was, said Leven, difficult to obtain information from the north, such was the general disaffection. As to the presbyterians, he thought that only 'McMillan's fools', the Cameronians, were a danger. (But would presbyterians have fought against their king? Ker of Kersland, in an attempt to wring some money out of government the following year, maintained that the Cameronians for their part would have done so. His purpose made his pleading suspect; so the authorities seem to have thought, and the Cameronians went unpaid.) But Scotland's leading presbyterian peer, the Duke of Atholl, was known to have been implicated with so many others of the nobility and gentry. They had now all to be ingathered, and a special effort had to be made to secure Atholl quickly.

Leven sent an emissary to Blair Castle whither the duke had retired from his more accessible house near Dunkeld. The messenger was denied access to the castle and informed that the duke 'was about his private business'. Leven persisted. Atholl pleaded sickness. Leven sent a Lieutenant Campbell and a party of soldiers to billet themselves at Blair. This they did to the indignation of the duke who complained over Leven's head to the Earl of Mar that his convalescence could not progress because 'the soldiers are quartered below the bedchamber

James III and VIII, attributed to Francesco Trevisani, said to have
been painted in 1708. From the Collection at Stanford Hall, near
Rugby; photograph: Courtauld Institute of Art.

'Advance, illustrious JAMES THE EIGHT
Now take possession of your right,
Old Albion for you declares, for you declares,
The rebel rogues confounded are with fears,
Scotland unite 'gainst all, 'gainst all that dare oppose,
Fight, fight and overcome your King's and Country's foes.
*A song at the time of the invasion 1708 to the tune of 'Britons Strike
Home'* – The Lockhart Papers I 501.

where I lie'. Atholl also protested that he had known nothing of the attempt from France:

> His Duchess (who was a person of eminent merit and very dear to him) deceasing, he resolved to retire, and accordingly having gone home he by his retirement and grief turned hectic and knew so little of what was doing in the world that the first account he had of the late intended invasion was from the public reports when it drew very near and flagrant.

It was as well that His Grace was not examined under oath on this.

Atholl by reason of his protestations of ill-health was permitted to remain at home on a hefty bond of presentation. So were Strathmore and the elderly Breadalbane, both likewise suddenly unwell. But thanks to the information provided to government over the past year by Ker of Kersland and suchlike there was now almost, but not quite, a clean sweep of the other Jacobite nobility and gentry who had lent their names to the invitation to the King of France of the previous year. Of the peers, in addition to the three above-mentioned invalids there were the Duke of Gordon and his son Huntly; the Earls of Seaforth, Traquair, Nithsdale, Errol, Moray, Aberdeen, Panmure and the Earl Marischal; Viscounts Stormont, Kilsyth and Kenmure; Lord John Drummond, Lord Nairne, Lord Sinclair from Fife and Lord Saltoun from Buchan. There were a score of gentlemen, notably the Angus laird, Fotheringham of Powrie, who had so greatly assisted Colonel Hooke while on his travels. Even Fletcher of Saltoun, though he had had no hand in the plotting, was arrested. Of 'the little gentlemen of the Highlands' as Leven derisively termed them, there were the venerable Sir Ewen Cameron of Lochiel and his son, McDonnell of Keppoch, Sir Donald MacDonald of Sleat, Stewart of Appin, Robertson of Struan, and the Captain of Clanranald who surrendered himself to Major-General Maitland and his small garrison at Fort William. Glengarry, who had taken to the hills, still remained outwith the net.

All these were housed in some congestion in Edinburgh castle and at Stirling, though Leven, 'the civilest man alive' as Lockhart his political adversary would concede, did his best to mitigate their discomfort, and in so doing won their good opinions. In April and early May all were shipped to London for whatever retribution government might think fit to devise.

It was the Duke of Hamilton who now saved the day. In character, he had skipped out of direct implication in the '08 (as it would come to be known in Scotland to distinguish it from those later Jacobite adventures, the '15, the '19, and the '45). A month and a half before Forbin's ships appeared in the Forth he had learned from his own sources of intelligence that invasion would come. The news found him at the home of a kinsman in Tweeddale where he and his duchess had paused on their way from his house at Kinneil on the Forth to her great Lancashire estates. Lockhart of Carnwath was with the duke when the news came; the latter's response to it was vintage Hamilton. 'If, after I have come so far with my family, I do all of a sudden return back', he said, 'everybody will conclude it is with a design to join the King, and so I shall be exposed to the malice of my enemies'. Better to go on to England where word of the king's landing could reach him within two or three days of it happening and he could immediately force his way north.

Then the duke thought of a still better reason for not turning back. 'The people of Scotland are all ready enough to join the King at the instant he lands', he said. 'I do not know but I may do him better service by being in the north of England to excite his friends there to appear for him'. And so it was settled. Lockhart was to go back to Lanarkshire and raise Hamilton's people, and his own, when the king landed. They would march south to join the duke at Dumfries where, he said, warming to his theme, they would 'thus be in condition to defend the Borders of Scotland against any attempt from England until a Scots army was formed, the Parliament convened, and the King's affairs settled'. With the prospect of the leading role this would have given him in the Stuart restoration, Hamilton may even have been sincere, as Lockhart clearly thought he was; but his Grace had also kept his options open.

On Fleming's arrival in Scotland in late February with word that invasion was on the way, a 'Mr John Hamilton, son to Mr Hamilton of Wishaw', rode south in haste to inform the duke at his Lancashire house. The duke thereupon,

> sat up three nights expecting every moment the other express with the account of the King's being actually landed, in which case he was resolv'd with about forty horses to have rid night and day, and forced his way from the messenger (his Grace being put in Messenger's hands upon the first account of the invasion, by orders of the Council of England) and thro' the country, till he had reached Scotland . . .

But when word came from Scotland it was of the failure of the invasion.

Hamilton was thus sufficiently non-involved in the whole affair – so far as Queen Anne's ministers knew – for him to make his intervention when the Jacobite peers and nobility were shipped to London in the April and May of 1708 – 'like hoggs to market' said Lockhart. The duke was likewise brought as a prisoner to London, but sensing the discord between the power-hungry Whigs and Godolphin the Queen's first minister, he made contact with the former and prevailed on them to obtain his own liberation and that of the Scottish nobility and gentry, now under threat, on their engaging to join with the Whigs and their friends in Scotland in the elections about to take place for the sixteen Scottish representative peers in the parliament of Great Britain.

'This' said Lockhart, 'certainly was one of the nicest steps the Duke of Hamilton ever made, and had he not hit upon this favourable juncture and managed it with great address, I am afraid some heads had paid for it'. At Versailles, learning that the Jacobite nobility and gentry were to get off, as it were, Scot-free, Saint-Simon marvelled at the wisdom of the British queen and the temperate behaviour of her ministers; but he did not know the inside story.

There remained the embarrassing presence in captivity of the aged English cavalier peer Lord Griffin and the awkward question of what to do with the Stirlingshire gentry who had raised their following too soon on the rumour that the king had landed. Lord Griffin, one of the court at St Germain, had not been privy to the invasion plan. Learning of it only in late February he borrowed a hundred louis d'or from his friend the Comte de Toulouse, bought a horse, and rode to Dunkirk. A place was found for him as a passenger, along with the Earl of Middleton's two sons, on *Le Salisbury*. When the Chevalier de Nangis struck her colours in the action off the Angus coast in the early hours of Sunday 14th March, along with Lieutenant-General the Marquis de Lévy and four hundred French infantry, he became a prisoner, but one taken in an act of open rebellion; and so his head was in danger. Of the Queen's ministers, the Earl of Sunderland in particular was for exacting the supreme penalty; but Anne who had known the old nobleman all her life – he had been a lieutenant-colonel in the Guards – would have none of it. He was respited again and again until weight of years rather than the headsman's axe finished him off.

No such sentimentality was likely to save the Stirlingshire gentry. Ministers were anxious to make an example of these half-dozen gentlemen and their following who had made their way through Perthshire to join the king in the mistaken belief that he had landed somewhere north of the Tay. The innkeepers along the route they had taken – at Brig o' Turk and Lochearnhead, at Appin of Dull in Strathtay and at Dunkeld – had little to say about them. It was true that the gentlemen from Stirlingshire had red clothes and cloaks, swords and pistols and had been heard to drink 'their master's health'; but like the others, the Menzies changehouse keeper at Appin of Dull 'was but seldom with them and heard little of their discourse'. The prosecution then sought to deploy some who would turn King's evidence to save their own skins, but the bench held that the law of Scotland forbade the evidence of those who were *socii criminis*, equally guilty; and a servant of James Stirling of Keir, one of the lairds on trial, when questioned under oath could not remember anything of their military parade which had preceded the escapade.

The outcome was a verdict of 'not proven'. Teased by his master on his perjury as they rode homewards from the trial, the servant with the poor memory responded with words still remembered by the Stirlings of Keir well over a century later: 'My mind was clear to trust my soul to the mercy o' heaven rather than your honour's body to the mercy of the Whigs'.

Parliament, righteously indignant at the shifty Scots, consoled itself by imposing the English law of treason north of the border; this would give government power to pick pliant judges for treason trials. It also passed an Act empowering Justices of the Peace to tender an oath 'of abjuration of the Pretender' to suspected persons. And Parliament pondered a measure, which it might better have completed, to discharge clansmen from their obligation to follow chiefs in rebellion against government.

The cover-up was effective; and the ill-success of the Jacobite Rising of 1715 would efface the memory of the '08. It would be forgotten that there had been in the earlier would-be insurrection active support from much of presbyterian Scotland instead of the well-organised opposition which the Earl of Mar and the Pretender encountered in 1715; that Stirling castle, the bulwark of government counter-measures seven years later, had been ripe for picking in 1708.

Though many of the families who had been implicated in the '08 took part, the '15 always had a look of failure about it. An international context in which Scotland could bargain her way back to independence did not exist. Before it erupted, in the last years of Queen Anne, with the nation wearying of the war and the Tories come into power, it had seemed more and more to the optimists of St Germain that a peaceful Stuart succession would be engineered when the queen's health finally gave out. In the complicated story which tells how this did not happen and how the Whigs and the House of Hanover prevailed, there was no doubt a certain widespread distaste in England for the Stuart claimant who had allowed himself to be made a tool of French designs in 1708. But that was not the real obstacle. It was James' refusal to embrace the protestant faith which, as always, was his undoing.

Even so, mysterious to the end, the Duke of Hamilton had put it about that he would top his success in freeing the conspirators of the '08 by acting the kingmaker to young James. Hamilton had prospered in the later years of Queen Anne, being awarded both an English dukedom and the Garter. This was followed by his nomination by the queen as ambassador-extraordinary to Versailles now that peace with France was coming. It was widely conjectured that his mission would be to bring about a Stuart succession to the throne of Great Britain; and in leaving Scotland to take up this post the duke conveyed to Lockhart of Carnwath, still his disciple and friend, that this was his purpose. Shortly afterwards, before he could leave London for Versailles, he was slain in the notorious duel with Lord Mohun over the disposal of the duchess's fortune. The Lancashire inheritance did for his Grace, just as it had done for old Scotland.

Last in this review of the Scottish *dramatis personae* there is Simon, 12th Lord Lovat, he who had first hit on playing the Scottish card and whose malign proceedings had in the event done so much to prevent it being played to effect. When Queen Anne died he returned to Scotland from France, switching sides adroitly to hold Inverness and thereabouts for King George against the Jacobites; thereby winning royal pardon for all past offences and the leadership of his clan. His character did not change, and right up to his death on Tower Hill in 1746, his long life bore this out. A quarter of a century on from the ripping of my lady's stays at Castle Dounie, and by then the undisputed 12th Lord Lovat, he settled a dispute with a kinsman by hiring some desperadoes from Lochiel's country to hack the legs off his cousin's cattle. Some years after this it was he who had the inconvenient Lady Grange abducted to exile on St Kilda. There was another side to him – there always had been – as the Revd. Alexander Carlyle would remember when in 1741 he saw him at his ease in a tavern near Edinburgh, up-staging the company by pronoucing the Grace in French, then merrily dancing a reel with the landlady's pretty daughter though his own legs were 'as thick as posts'. This more genial aspect of his character did not quell the frenzy of ambition four years later in which he forced his reluctant heir to join the '45 to the loss of lands, title, and his own grey head.

What if the '08 had succeeded? What if, with the north of England under Scottish occupation, London shivering for lack of Tyne coal, and the towns of Flanders in revolt, the Allies had been forced to a peace with France from which Scotland emerged independent once more and with young James as king? On this it has to be said that while Scotland might have found in the stress of events a unity which she had rarely enjoyed before (or since) her underlying economic weakness would have remained unchanged; success in the '08 could have proved a barren victory for a Scotland excluded from trade with England's empire. It is still more likely that, eventually quelled by an angered and vindictive England, Scotland would have been placed in the subordinate and unhappy position of Ireland with consequences as lamentable as those that befell the sister island. So, on the failure of the '08 the verdict has to be that in the short-term for Scotland the Union was the lesser of two evils, a thought which perhaps was in Sir Walter Scott's mind in writing *The Black Dwarf*: Hobbie Elliot to the martially-minded Jacobite gentry urging them to 'gang home quietly'.

'. . . there's sure news come frae London that him they ca' Bang or Byng or what is't, has bang'd the French ships and the new King aft the coast . . . sae, ye had best bide content wi' auld Nanse for want of a better Queen'.

And in the longer perspectives of history? In the Memoirs of that arch-scoundrel the Laird of Kersland, there is one passage of remembered conversation which rings true. In it the Duke of Queensberry in pressing Ker to act as his secret agent argued persuasively that the Union must work, because it would always be in the interests of England to make it work. If that is indeed still true today then we may perhaps be grateful that the Union with England survived, and that the Auld Alliance between France and Scotland was drowned at sea off the East Neuk of Fife on the morning of 13th March 1708.

# Appendix

*A brief account of the War in the year one thousand Seven Hundred and Eight*
by John Scott, souldier
[*From The Remembrance. A metrical Account of the War in Flanders 1701–12* reproduced in Appendix II to Vol III of *The Scots Brigade in the Service of the United Netherlands*, Scottish History Society, 1899]

Now of the seven hundered and eight,
   My purposse is for to relate.
The Pope and French King did plot and combine
   All Protesstants for to defeatte.
And for that designe they plot and combine
   A popish King to enthrone.
In the Isle Britan to make an invassion,
   They have condeshended upon.
King James the third their oun true blood,
   A sword they put in his hand.
With Frenchmen aneue and Irish men true,
   That hosst he got to comande
The shipping right good they did him provide,
   And with him good Generalls three.
Then that Navie of French men of war,
   At Dunkirk made ready for sea.
The Prince of Walles to conquer these Isles,
   Set out with courage most stout.
And all his Navie to guard him at sea,
   Till England they compast about.
The Churchmen in France their joy to advance,
   Was nou in devotion most fervant.
With humble masses and double adresses,
   Processions for the purpose subservant.
Both late and soon their mussick bells rang,
   And clergie men racked to church.
To make intercession for the holy profession,
   Which they thought was promotted by such.
The Britans union they thought was broken,
   Their oun Native King called home.
And the French Navie was saffe over sea,

And the King was set on his throne.
And throu Flanders it was the tideings,
  That the French, Scotland did invade.
And twelve regiments marched from Flanders,
  Without any longer abade.
And at Hostend right soon they got shiping,
  And saffely past throu the sea.
And at Neucassel they lay at an anchor,
  Al ready to give them suplie.
The French Navie ran to the North sea,
  And near the Coast of Scotland.
The Dutch and English fleet perseued after that,
  And instantlie came on that bande.
It came to passe not far from the Basse,
  A sea feight hapened to be.
Near the Coast of Scotland the Frenchies did stand
  Til at length they were forced to flee.
With cruel like pride and many a broad side,
  The battel was managed a while,
And the Dutch fleet stod very weel by it,
  And the battel was fought without guile.
Til the French Navie was broken on sea,
  And scatered from thence abroad.
And on that uncouth coast was cruely tosst,
  Coming off in many a roade.
What ships were sunke and what were burnt,
  I shal not now tel to you.
Bot Captan Gordoun that day got tane,
  A French ship and her whole crewe.
The Scotish men was now gathering,
  To defend themselves on the land.
Some of the French was tane prissoners,
  And delivered saffe to their hand.
The Prince of Wailles with broken sailles,
  Came stealing back to France.
And at Dunkirk came saffe to land,
  After that sudene mischance.
Up that countrie right fast passed he,
  And the nixt day vent to the messe.
With the French armie to camp vent he
  In hopes of some better sucsesse.
These tideing then to Flanders came,
  That the French was beat on the sea.
The third of Apriele our garissones all

Fired for the great victorie
In Coutridge toun all the garissoune,
   Did keep the Queen's birth day.
And our General had a noble caball,
   And the musickes sweetlie did play.
And at the State housse that old antient place,
   Two lantrons was made to give light.
With hunders of candels burning into those,
   Which was a great shew on that night.
Each several torch of these sumptuous lantrons.
   Of diverse collours was dyeed.
And in al the windous was burning candels,
   Throu the Market place as we hyeed.

# Notes and Sources

The two large parchment-covered folio volumes from Hooke's Franco-Jacobite papers, deposited in the Bodleian Library in 1816, were edited for the Roxburghe Club by William D. Macray and published in two volumes as *The Correspondence of Colonel Nathaniel Hooke* in 1870–1 (cited hereafter as *Hooke I* and *Hooke II*). The originals are mostly written in a neat regular hand and contain transcripts of more than seven hundred letters and memoranda from 1702 onwards, ending abruptly at the close of 1707. Marginal comment indicates that they were sifted by Hooke with the help of his nephew, also a Nathaniel Hooke, who later became a well-known literary figure in Dr Johnson's England. The task seems to have been begun in 1716, significantly the year which saw the collapse of another Jacobite attempt.

The preface to *Hooke I* reproduces a letter from 1739 (the year after Hooke's death) to Nathaniel (the nephew) from a cousin, indicating that Hooke's papers included more than the two manuscript volumes lodged with the Bodleian, and that there were amongst them papers of 1708 dealing with the actual conduct of the invasion-attempt of that year. Some of these, like the Bodleian manuscripts, seem to have survived the visit of a Court official in 1740, intent on suppressing Hooke's revelations. The evidence for this is the publication at the Hague in 1758 (when a later invasion of Britain from France was under consideration) of a volume in French containing some of the material now in *Hooke II* as well as other papers concerning the March 1708 attempt. Translated editions appeared in London, Edinburgh and Dublin in 1760 under the title *The Secret History of Colonel Hooke's Negociations in Scotland in favour of the Pretender in 1707. Including the Original Letters and Papers which passed between the Scotch and Irish Lords and the Courts at Versailles and St. Germains. Never before published. Written by himself. With a translation of the letters containing a Narrative of the Pretender's Expedition into Scotland in 1708 and his Return to Dunkirk, transmitted to the French Court by the Commanding Officers of the Squadron.* I refer to this as *Hooke's Negociations*. It is not clear whether Nathaniel the nephew, or someone else, was the editor.

Macray correctly surmised that some of the papers actually impounded by the Court in 1740 might have survived, and from the Ministère des Affaires Etrangères in Paris he obtained a list of these which was reproduced as appendix C to *Hooke II*.

Prof. Claude Nordmann in his chapter 'Louis XIV and the Jacobites' in *Louis XIV and Europe* ed. Ragnhild Hatton (London, 1976) draws attention to the records in the Archives de la Guerre, the Archives Nationales and the Archives de la Marine in Paris which reflect Hooke's efforts and in particular bring out the extent of military planning from 1703 onwards to bring them to fruit.

Hooke's report of his mission to Scotland in 1707, which is one of the items in both *Hooke II* and *Hooke's Negociations*, was mostly reproduced in *The*

*Chevalier de St. George and the Jacobite Movements*, edited by C. S. Terry in 1901 (2nd edition, London 1915). This excerpt also appears in Terry's *The Jacobites and the Union* (Cambridge University Press 1922).

All dates are expressed in the Old Style, i.e. according to the Julian calendar in use in Britain until 1752. This has meant a deduction of eleven days from dates used by Hooke and other French sources, since these conformed to the Gregorian calendar.

## PREAMBLE: THE BRAES OF KILLIECRANKIE
This is based on the memoir of the battle written shortly after the event by the defeated commander (Maj. Gen. Hugh MacKay; *Memoirs of the War Carried on in Scotland and in Ireland 1689–1691*; Edinburgh, 1833)

p 1 Dutch troops, uniform of Scots Brigade; *The Scots Brigade in Holland*, vol. I (Scottish History Society, Edinburgh 1899), p 2 battle in Lochaber; the battle of Mulroy 1688, 'the last big clan battle', in which with the help of the Camerons the MacDonells of Keppoch defeated Clan Mackintosh and government troops.

## THE CONSPIRATORS
### 1. NATHANIEL HOOKE
p 9 'the ruffle at Killiecrankie'; R. Chambers, *Domestic Annals of Scotland* (3 vols, Edinburgh 1861) III 47. p 9 use of torture; *ibid.* III 40. p 10 Hooke's early life; *Hooke II* preface; *Dictionary of National Biography.* p 11 with Dundee; *Hooke I* 48. p 11 in Monmouth's rebellion; C. Chevenix-Trench, *The Western Rising* (London 1969) *passim.* p 12 James rejoices; L. Norton (ed) *Historical Memoirs of the Duc de Saint-Simon* (3 vols, London 1967) I 9. p 12 in French service; *Hooke II* preface; *DNB*; J. C. O'Callaghan, *History of the Irish Brigades in the Service of France* (Glasgow 1886), p 14 papers impounded; *Hooke I* vif. p 14 Versailles; *Saint-Simon* (ed. Norton) I 15f. p 14 Chamillart; *Biographie Universelle Ancienne et Moderne*, Paris 1857. p 14 the king's council; J. C. Rule, 'Colbert de Torcy' in R. Hatton (ed.) *Louis XIV and Europe* (London 1976) 278. p 14 the 'global view'; *Hooke I* 1–21. p 17 'mémoire sur les affaires d'Écosse'; *ibid.* 21–39. G. M. Trevelyan, *Ramillies and the Union with Scotland* (London 1932) says that 'Hooke never realized that the strength of the Jacobite fighting force lay in the Highland clans, about whom he made few enquiries'; but cf. *Hooke I* 34 and the many other assessments in his papers of the military potential of the clans which show that (particularly in the light of Killiecrankie) he took their support and potential for granted (e.g. his discussion with Middleton quoted p 32 below). p 18 the Scottish exiles; J. Browne, *A History of the Highlands and of the Highland Clans* (4 vols, Glasgow 1838) I 197–210 (Sir Walter Scott's *Tales of a Grandfather*, chp. LVII had given a shorter version of the episode).

### 2. SIMON FRASER
p 22 the Lovat inheritance, the rape, the 'Scots Plot'; the many sources, some of which are reproduced in Terry, *Chevalier*, chp. II, are distilled in B. Lenman, *The Jacobite Clans of the Great Glen, 1650–1784* (London 1984) 57–73. p 21 meets Louis XIV; H. K. Fraser (ed.) *Memoirs of the Life of Simon, Lord Lovat, written by himself in the French language and now first translated from the original manuscript [London 1797]* (London 1902) 97f. p 22 Amelia

Reoch; Hugo Arnot, *A Collection and Abridgement of Celebrated Criminal Trials in Scotland* (Edinburgh 1785) 89. p 24 Middleton; *D N B*. Middleton had come over to St Germain in 1693, having been caught in correspondence with that court. p 30 Hooke and Fraser's mission; Fraser arrived in Paris towards the end of 1702. Hooke's 'global view of the war' was written in February 1703 and his 'mémoire sur les affaires d'Écosse' in December. He confesses (*Hooke I* 51) to having had meetings with Fraser but disclaims detailed knowledge of his project (though this is highly questionable). p 27 Scotland under arms; *The Memoirs of John Ker Esq.*, *of Kersland* (London 1727); elsewhere there is much contemporary evidence of serious military training. p 28 Lovat's return to Paris; *Hooke I* 112–143. p 34 King's College records; Alexd. Fergusson (ed.) *Major Fraser's Manuscript* (2 vols, Edinburgh 1889) II appendix 1.

## 3. JAMES, 4TH DUKE OF HAMILTON

p 35 Blenheim; G. S. Stevenson (ed.) *The Letters of Madame (The correspondence of Elizabeth-Charlotte of Bavaria)* (2 vols London 1924) I 237. p 35 the Scottish project revived; *Hooke I* 157–249. p 38 *L'Audacieuse*; *ibid.* 249–52. p 40 reports to the council; *ibid.* 372–428. p 41 at Slains; *ibid.* 372f. p 42 arrives at Edinburgh; *ibid.* 374. p 43 at Comiston; *ibid.* 375. In literature the 4th duke appears as a grand heroic figure in *Henry Esmond*, but he has so far escaped the attention of biographers. There is a perceptive assessment in R. Marshall, *The Days of Duchess Anne* (London 1973) chp. 10. p 43 'I must distinguish between his principles and his Popery'; *Proceedings of the Estates in Scotland* (2 vols, Scottish History Society, Edinburgh 1955) II 297. p 45 Lockhart's view; G. Lockhart of Carnwath, *Memoirs Concerning the Affairs of Scotland from Queen Anne's Accession to the Throne . . . to the Union* (London 1714) 28. p 45 Clerk's view; *Memoirs of the Life of Sir John Clerk of Penicuik, Bart.* (Scottish History Society, Edinburgh 1892) 57f. p 46 Hooke meets Countess Marischal, Earl Marischal and Errol; *Hooke I* 375–82. p 47 first moves to Union; W. Ferguson, *Scotland's Relations with England; A Survey to 1707* (Edinburgh 1977) which incidentally brings out how little expectation there was in Scotland that anything would ever come of the Union proposals. For the general Union background see B. Lenman, *The Jacobite Risings in Great Britain 1689–1746* (London, 1980) and P. W. J. Riley *The Union of England and Scotland* (London, 1978). p 48 first meeting with Hamilton; I have limited myself to necessary abridgement and where appropriate, changed indirect to direct speech. As an example, here is Hooke's narrative of part of his first meeting with the duke:

> Madame de Largo m'aiant quitté à la porte de sa chambre, je trouvay le Duc, qui m'attendoit sans lumière; il m'embrassa avec beaucoup d'affection, m'appellant son camarade de prison, nous avions eté prisonniers ensemble dans la Tour de Londres il y a plus de seize ans. Je reconnus sa voix d'abord. Il commença par me dire les raisons qui l'avoient obligé à me recevoir d'une maniere si extraordinaire; qu'il ne se fioit à personne; que tous ses amis qui avoient connoissance de mon voyage luy viendroient demander s'il m'avoit vû, qu'ainsi il vouloit être en etat d'affirmer par serment que non; et qu'au reste il avoit dessein de me parler sans reserve, et que je n'avois qu'à luy dire les propositions dont j'etois chargé.
> Je luy fis la même reponse qu'au Comte d'Erroll, ajoutant que la Reyne

d'Angleterre dans sa lettre avoit assez expliqué le sujet de ma mission, et que je m'attendois à des propositions de sa part.

Il me repondit, que la Reyne d'Angleterre croit les choses plus meures qu'elles ne sont; et que dans le fond elle ne peut l'assurer du secours, qu'il n'y a que le Roy qui le peut promettre, et qu'il s'etonnoit de ce que sa Majesté n'avoit pas envoyé vers eux l'année derniere.

Je repondis que, le Roy n'ayant pas besoin des Ecossois, il ne devoit pas s'en étonner que sa Majesté avoit été informée qu'ils demandoient sa protection; que là dessus elle m'avoit ordonné de me transporter en Ecosse pour sçavoir ce qui en est; que j'avois ordre de m'adresser principalement à luy, et que s'il vouloit agir franchement avec moy j'agirois de même avec luy.

Il me demanda si je n'avois pas une lettre de creance. Je repondis que j'avois une lettre du Roy à luy rendre, mais qu'étant sans lumiere, il ne la pouvoit lire; à ces mots il se leva, me disant que les tenebres m'empechoient de voir sur son visage combien il étoit touché de l'honneur que le Roy luy faisoit, qu'il en étoit tout penetré, et qu'il me prioit tres instamment de luy donner la lettre de sa Majesté. Je luy dis que je luy donnerois non seulement la lettre du Roy, mais que je luy ferois voir que j'etois assez authorisé pour prendre toutes les mesures necessaires pour le bien de l'Ecosse, et pour son avantage en particulier. Il prit la lettre et mon pouvoir, et passa dans un autre chambre pour les lire. Puis m'étant revenu trouver il me rendit mon pouvoir, et me dit qu'il feroit garder la lettre de Sa Majesté dans les archives de sa maison; que le Roy luy avoit fait trop d'honneur, et qu'il tâcheroit d'y repondre le mieux qu'il luy seroit possible.

p 53 second meeting with Hamilton; *ibid.* I 393-8. p 56 meets Marischal, Errol, Home, bishop of Edinburgh etc.; *ibid*. I 398-401. p 57 meets Lockhart; Lockhart, *Memoirs* 197f. p 57 third meeting with Hamilton; *Hooke I* 405-9. p 57 duchess's bedchamber; for information about the furnishings of the ducal apartments I am indebted to Mr Ian McIvor, Principal Inspector of Ancient Monuments in Scotland. p 61 fourth meeting with Hamilton; *Hooke I* 416-8. p 62 Hamilton's *volte-face*; Lockhart, *Memoirs* 169-77. The evidence in *Hooke I* for Hamilton's motives falls into place alongside Dr William Ferguson's summing-up (*op. cit.* 230f) and the discussion of other evidence of Hamilton's subversion by the Court in P. H. Scott, *1707: The Union of Scotland and England* (Edinburgh 1979) 35-8. Trevelyan (*op. cit.* 278) to some extent makes light of the reality of Scottish opposition to the Union, just as he seems to have taken not quite seriously the threat of uprising in 1708, but his summing-up of Hamilton's political *persona* will surely not be bettered (p 278). The Hamilton muniments (Scottish Record Office GD 406/1) contain some interesting sidelights on Hamilton's conduct in 1705, from Home's exhortation to the duke to 'bestirre himself' and 'preserve our poor country from slavery which is so much in danger at present by our proud and ambitious neighbour nation' to Duchess Anne's bewilderment: '. . . as to your politicks, truely I understand none of them'. In a letter to his mother of 1 September 1707 he offers a bare-faced excuse for his own *volte-face*: 'I am now resolved to lay down the cudgell and acknowledge I am beaten since the country [Country Party?] would do nothing to preserve its own interests when uniting with England'. (I am grateful to Dr Rosalind Marshall who catalogued the Hamilton papers for guidance through them.)

p 63 Carnegy's letters; *Hooke I* 334–6. p 64 in the north; *ibid.* I 421f. p 65 provisioning of *L'Audacieuse*; *ibid.* I 339. p 65 returns to France; *ibid.* I 423. p 65 his conclusions; *ibid.* I 424–8. p 66 Fleming goes to France; *ibid.* II 1–13, p 66 Clerk on the *volte-face*; Clerk, *Memoirs* 57–8. p 67 Lady Errol's view; *Hooke II* 37ff.

### 4. GEORGE LOCKHART OF CARNWATH

Lockhart's *Memoirs* (already cited) were reproduced in *The Lockhart Papers: Containing Memoirs and Commentaries upon the Affairs of Scotland from 1702 to 1715, by George Lockhart Esq. of Carnwath* . . . (2 vols, London 1817) vol. I. Daniel Defoe's secret correspondence with Harley, first published in 1897 by the Historical Manuscripts Commission, is reproduced in G. H. Healey (ed.) *The Letters of Daniel Defoe* (Oxford 1955). The complex story of the armed opposition to Union in the autumn and winter of 1706 and how it came to nothing can (to some extent) be unravelled from these notoriously 'loaded' sources, together with *The Memoirs of John Ker Esq. of Kersland* (3 vols, London 1727). Andrew Lang's considered opinion was that the threat of armed insurrection was glaring, and only averted by the machinations of government and the Duke of Hamilton (A. Lang, *History of Scotland*, 4 vols, Edinburgh 1900–7; vol. IV 123–131).

p 68 Clerk remembers; Clerk, *Memoirs* 58. p 69 Hooke at Menin; *Hooke II* Hooke's insistence that he made no mention of his Scottish mission the previous year is to be noted: the gossip in Edinburgh (Lockhart, *Memoirs*, 198) apparently was that he had been less than discreet. p 70 the Lockharts; S. MacDonald Lockhart, *Seven Centuries: A History of the Lockharts of Lee and Carnwath* (privately published 1976). p 71 Lockhart as a commissioner; Lockhart, *Memoirs*, 185–191. p 71 Queen Anne's letter; *A Collection of the Parliamentary Debates in England from the year MDCLXVIII* (1741), Vol V2. p 73 the Edinburgh scene and riots; Lockhart, *Memoirs*, 222–5. p 74 the killing of the captain of the *Worcester* seems to have been more generally approved of, e.g. by Lockhart himself, SRO GD 406/1, 9726. p 75 riots in Glasgow; Ferguson, *op. cit.* 267. p 75 Duchess Anne disapproves; Hamilton muniments *SRO* 9734, 5338. p 75 Defoe on the Glasgow riots; Defoe, *op. cit.* 163. p 75 the Cameronians at Dumfries; Lockhart, *Memoirs*, 273–7; Lang, *op. cit.* 127–8. p 77 attack on Argyll and Queensberry; Lockhart, *Memoirs* 252. p 77 Cunninghame of Aiket; *ibid.* 278–83. The minister of Dunlop parish, Ayrshire in *The New Statistical Account of Scotland* (Edinburgh 1845) describes Aiket castle as a square tower, vaulted on the ground floor, four to five storeys high, 'for centuries, home of a branch of the Cunninghames'. p 78 rendezvous at Hamilton; Lockhart, *Memoirs* 283f. p 78 Atholl's rising; D. Stewart, *Sketches of the Highlanders of Scotland* (2 vols, Edinburgh 1822) I 71 and n. p 78 petition to the queen; Lockhart, *Memoirs* 286–8. p 79 the inside story; *ibid.* 325f.

### 5. JOHN KER OF KERSLAND: COLONEL HOOKE RETURNS

Ker's *Memoirs* (already cited) were published in 1727: only vol. I concerns his doings in 1706–8.

p 83 Ker's antecedents; Malcolm Kerr, *Notices of the Family of Kerr of Kerrisland* (London 1880); James Paterson, *History of the County of Ayr with a genealogical account of the families of Ayrshire* (Ayr 1847). p 83 Ker's dealings, autumn 1706 to spring 1707; Ker, *Memoirs* 30 *et seq.* p 86 Defoe as Ker's 'controller'; *Letters* 163. Healey disputes Lang's identification of Ker as Defoe's spy among the Cameronians (Lang *op. cit.* 127–131) but Lang's reasoning remains impressive and Healey's objections seem insufficient. p 86 Ker meets Jacobites; Ker, *Memoirs* 40f. p 86 Lockhart on Ker; *Lockhart Papers* I. p 85 the Royal Warrant; Ker, *Memoirs* frontispiece. p 87 Hooke ordered to Scotland; *Hooke II* 152 et seq. p 87 at Slains; *ibid.* II 347–59. p 88 Ogilvie of Boyne; A & H Tayler *The Ogilvies of Boyne* (Aberdeen 1933). p 88 at Powrie; *Hooke.* II 359–60. p 88 Sinclair of Steventon ('le seigneur de Steenton' in the Bodleian original; 'D'Estevenson', evidently a mistake in transcription, in *Hooke II*) was a Lanarkshire laird related by marriage to the Lockharts and member of the Estates of Parliament for Lanarkshire. p 89 at Scone; *ibid.* II 365. p 89 Ker's letter; *ibid.* II 371–2. p 90 Lockhart on presbyterian support; Lockhart, *Memoirs* 343. Andrew Lang (*op. cit.* 124–5) describes amusingly his attempt eighty years ago to persuade the Free Church of Scotland, custodians of the Cameronian records, to disclose what evidence there was of Ker of Kersland's leadership of the Cameronian sects. The Cameronians soon became embarrassed at having been led by such a scoundrel as Kersland and they too 'covered-up'; but, as Lang brings out, the evidence is clear that Ker had indeed enjoyed a position of influence among them.

## THE ATTEMPT ON SCOTLAND:
### 1. L'ENTREPRISE D'ECOSSE

The abridged translation of Saint-Simon's *Memoirs* by Lucy Norton (already cited) omits some relevant passages which appear in Bayle St John, *The Memoirs of the Duke de St Simon abridged from the French* (London, 1857). For the full range of Saint-Simon's very full account of *L'entreprise d'Ecosse* it is necessary to go to the complete text: A. de Boislisle, *Mémoires de Saint-Simon* (41 vols, Paris 1901) XV. References to Saint-Simon in these successive chapters are from pages 401–435.

p 93 the Memorial: *Hooke II* 256–62, and also *Hooke's Negociations* 69–75. p 97 return to Dunkirk: *Hooke II* 410. p 98 report to French Ministers: *ibid.* II 347–409, and *Hooke's Negociations* 5–68. The strategy of cutting off London's coal supply may have had its origins in the Scottish occupation of Newcastle in 1640: London had also shivered in the winter of 1643 when Newcastle was in royalist hands. p 97 James expected: Lockhart, *Memoirs* 358. p 98 at Versailles: *Hooke II* 416. p 98 Chevreuse helps: *ibid.* 424. p 98 plan given to Chamillart *ibid.* 431–33. p 100 new civil service: Lockhart, *Memoirs* 342. p 100 Hamilton's letter; *Hooke's Negociations* 83–6. p 101 Ker's letter; *ibid.* 106f. p 101 Duchess of Gordon's letter: *ibid.* 107f. p 101 Ker unmasked: *Hooke II* 517, also 481, 523. p 101 Defoe's warnings: *Defoe op. cit.* 229 et seq. p 103 progress of Scottish project; *Hooke II* 482–86. p 103 Louis' distaste; *Saint-Simon* (Boislisle) XV 401. p 103 French view of the Union: *Saint-Simon* (Norton) I 323. p 103 James Ogilvie; *Hooke II* 501 et seq. p 104 the project approved: Saint-Simon (Boislisle) XV 408. p 104 Capt. Ogilvie's reports: *HMC* 15th Report, App Part IV.

### 2. THE COMTE DE FORBIN

Another spectator of events at Versailles, though less in the know than Saint-

Simon, was the Marquis de Dangeau. His *Journal* Vol XII, (Paris 1857) records the fortunes of the Scottish project from his first awareness in mid-February 1708.

Hooke's correspondence as reproduced in *Hooke I and II* ends abruptly with the last days of December 1707. Presumably the official from the French Foreign Ministry, seeking to impound 'official secrets' of the invasion attempt of thirty-two years before simply lifted all the papers he could find which bore a 1708 date. However, as noted earlier, *Hooke's Negociations* goes some considerable way towards making good what had been taken, and includes 'after-action' reports by some of the military and naval participants in the invasion attempt. It is not clear whether Hooke himself had copies of these, or whether the editor of *Hooke's Negociations* obtained them independently. Supplementing these reports are the *Mémoires de Claude, Comte de Forbin* (Paris 1731) an English translation of which appeared very soon afterwards (*Memoirs of Claude, Comte de Forbin*, London 1731). Forbin was still alive in 1731, and there is no doubt that the bluff quarrelsome tone of the Memoirs catches him to the life. They are particularly valuable in that they make it all too clear that Forbin had failed to grasp, or had not been told of, France's desperate strategic need in 1708 to set Scotland alight. Saint-Simon, shrewd observer of events, saw this with stark clarity: Forbin, admiral in command of the invasion fleet, did not! Forbin's biography, *Vie du Comte de Forbin, chef d'escadre des armées navales de France* by M. Richer '*auteur de plusiers onvrages de Littérature*' (Paris 1785) is disappointing and uninformative.

This apart, the veracity of the Memoirs is suspect. The *Biographie Générale Ancienne et Moderne* (Paris 1857) carries a lengthy entry on the admiral which accepts the Memoirs unquestioningly. However, Henri Malo (*La Grande Guerre des Corsaires, Dunkerque 1702–1715*, Paris 1925) points out that Forbin, an *officier rouge* of the king's navy, re-fashioned the record of his exploits at sea to his own greater glory and to the detriment of Malo's particular heroes, the *officiers bleus*, the professional privateering captains. In *War at Sea under Queen Anne* (Cambridge 1938) Commander J. H. Owen endorsed Malo's strictures. It was just such an adjustment to the record which Forbin perpetrated when he put the crucial and disastrous error in landfall on the Scottish coast at less than a score of miles when it was in fact a hundred. Such was the verve of the Memoirs that writers down the years from Sir Walter Scott to G.M. Trevelyan have accepted Forbin's version of events, although all the while there was a clear statement by Lockhart that landfall had been much, much further north.

Owen analysed the evidence of the Royal Navy's response to the invasion attempt as it is found in *The Byng Papers*, Vol. II (Publications of the Navy Records Society, Vol. LXVIII) and in the papers of the House of Lords enquiry of 1709 into the events of the previous year (*House of Lords MSS 17*, VIII new series 1708–10) to which there is a most useful introduction.

p 106 Forbin's return to Paris; *Biographie Générale* (Paris 1857). p 108 Forbin and Pontchartrain; Forbin, *Memoirs* (English version, cited above) 248–252. p 108 and Louis XIV; *ibid* 261f. p 108 duke of Berwick; C. Petrie, *The Marshal Duke of Berwick* (London 1953) *passim*. p 109 Voltaire's view; *Le Siècle de Louis XIV* (1751) chp. xxi. p 109 Petrie ascribed a March 1708 date to this memorandum, but it seems to have been of an earlier date while Berwick was still in Spain. It would have been natural for Louis to have consulted him so. There would have been no point in his urging the advantages of the landing on the Clyde from Brest when the expedition was on the very point of sailing from Dunkirk to the Forth.

p 111 balls at Versailles; Dangeau (above) Jan and Feb 1708 *passim*. p 112 Military preparations; *Hooke's Negociations* 121. p 112 Fleming's journey; *ibid*. 151 et seq. p 115 intelligence reports; *H of L Mss* (see above) 37f. p 115 speculation on invasion; Owen, *op cit. H of L Mss* 53. p 117 tussle in cabinet; E. Gregg, *Queen Anne* (London, 1980) chp 10. p 117 the Navy's response; Owen, *op. cit.* chp VIII, *H of L Mss* passim. p 118 Forbin tries to cancel; Forbin, *Memoirs* 264. An Italian translation of Louis' advice to James is at SM 3/24/8 in the Scottish Catholic Archives, Edinburgh p 119 Versailles waits; *Dangeau*, March 1708 *passim*. Forbin sails; *ibid*. 269. p 119 *Le Protée*; *Hooke's Negociations*. p 121 jacobite enthusiasm; Lockhart *Memoirs* 367, 373f. p 121 General Assembly; Defoe's *History*, preface. p 121 Leven's response; *H of L MSS* 140. p 121 dragoons at Dunbar; *ibid*. 139; the troop-commander was a Cornet David Ogilvie; I thought this might have been Harley's spy of the previous autumn, now given his reward, but it was not. p 122 *Analecta Scotica* (Edinburgh 1834) that collection of historical curios and rag-bag of bits and pieces contains what purports to be *A journal of the Dunkirk Squadron in their intended invasion against Scotland*. Internal evidence (the fact that some of its contents are manifestly wrong) suggests that it was a piece of opportunistic journalism of the time. p 122 where to land in Scotland?; *Hooke's Negociations* 140. p 123 Hooke sees the Aberdeenshire coast; *Hooke II* xv: this is a footnote provided by the editor, Macray, 'quoting from Oliphant's *Jacobite Lairds of Gask*, printed for the Grampian Club in 1870, p. 15':

General Hooke told Dr. King at Paris, that in the year 1708, when the French fleet made a show as if they intended to land in Scotland, he being one night not disposed to sleep, when about midnight on the deck, and as he was bred to the sea, (*sic*) saw they were stiring on Newcastle Bay; when he challenged the man at the helm, he answered he was going the course ordered; upon which the General went to the Commander to know the meaning of it, who came immediately on deck, reprimanded the stirsman severely, and ordered him to keep the proper course; being unable to rest, the General soon after returned to deck, and found they were again got upon the wrong course, and being told it was by direction, went instantly to the K . . .'s apartments, and telling him the story, said they were betrayed.

'Newcastle Bay' would be the bay of the New Castle of Slains (as distinct from Old Slains on the Aberdeenshire coast) which is known today as Cruden Bay. Among Hooke's papers impounded in 1740 and identified in the Foreign Ministry archives in Paris in 1870 are the '*Journal original de François Gavarry, le pilote de l'escadre de M. de Forbin*' and also, bearing the date 15 April 1708, '*Lettre de Gavarry à Hooke (Demande d'argent; écrite en anglais)*'. The copy of Gavarry's journal gives the correct date for departure from Dunkirk but puts the Aberdeenshire landfall at the morning of 11th March when it unquestionably was 12th March. Carelessness or cover-up? I am grateful to the Ministère des Affaires Etrangères for sending me copies of both, and mentioning that the correct reference is *Correspondence politique, Angleterre supplément, vol 4*.

p 123 off Stonehaven; *H of L Mss* 141. p 123 in Crail road; Forbin, *Memoirs* 270, *H of L MSS*. p 124 Byng watches Dunkirk; Owen, *op. cit.* 245. p 124 reaches the Forth; *ibid.* p 126 Berwick received by Louis; Petrie, *op. cit.* 222. p 126 Berwick's view; *ibid.* 225. p 127 the action off May Island; Owen, *op. cit.* 253. p 127 Chevalier de Nangis; Owen, (*op. cit.* 238) states that de Nangis, Forbin's senior captain, had visited Scotland to assess Jacobite strength in 1707. The source is not given, but a footnote to *Saint-Simon* (Boislisle, XV) denies it. p 128 James demands to be set ashore; Forbin, *Memoirs* 275f. There is an interesting anecdote by Sir Walter Scott (*Tales of a Grandfather*, chp. LXII) that James demanded to be landed at Wemyss castle (between Kirkcaldy and Leven on the Fife coast). I am assured by Dr Alice Wemyss that this is improbable: the then Earl of Wemyss was known to be pro-Union (as he would be, with his interest in the coal trade). From whence, then, did Scott get this anecdote? We may be sure he had some source for it. In general he followed Forbin's account, and it seems that he had also seen *Hooke's Negociations*. p 128 Forbin sails north; Forbin, *Memoirs* 278. p 129 dinner on *Le Mars*; Forbin, *Memoirs* 289. Forbin returns; Owen *op. cit.* 261f. p 129 James returns to Dunkirk; *H of L Mss* 47f. p 130 Forbin's Scottish antecedents; Forbin, *Memoirs* 279. p 130 letters from Byng at Leith; National Maritime Museum *MSS* AGC/15/band 7. I am indebted to the NMM for drawing attention to this p 131 Private Deane; Rev. J. B. Deane (ed.) *The Journal of Private J. M. Deane* (privately printed 1847).

For further guidance on ship movements in response to winds and tides I am indebted to Mr Peter Cooke of the School of Scottish Studies, Edinburgh University (who is also an ardent yachtsman).


3. THE COVER-UP

p 132 return of Le Zéphyr; *Hooke's Negociations*, 123. p 132 Bernières reports; *ibid.* 124–138. p 133 D'Andrezel's reports; *ibid.* 139–145. p 133 Matignon's report; *ibid.* 146–150. p 133 Forbin's excuse; Forbin, *Memoirs*, 270. p 134 Hooke's criticism; *Hooke Iv.* p 134 invasion planning in 1709; *Hooke II* Preface and Professor Nordmann's chapter in Hatton *op. cit.* p 134 James meets Louis XIV; The apocryphal story, perhaps intended to ridicule James, seems to stem from *The Memoirs of the Old Chevalier*, anon, London, 1712. It is repeated in Scott's *Tales of a Grandfather* and so has gained currency. But had it been true would not Dangeau and Saint-Simon have noted it? Their evidence runs the other way: *On ne fera point de cérémonies au roi d'Angleterre sur son chemin (Dangeau 92)* 13. The French court strove for secrecy. p 137 Voltaire's comment; *Le Siècle de Louis XIV* chp. xxi. p 137 his old age; Forbin, *Memoirs* 306.

The most explicit of Saint-Simon's several comments on the inner history of the '08 is in his note to Dangeau's *Journal* for March, 1708: 'This Scottish expedition was never liked by Portchartrain, hating Chamillart as he did. He was accused of having put all the obstacles in the way which he possibly could . . . Forbin was also accused of having had the opportunity to keep clear of the English on the coasts of Scotland and disembark everything. That the whole business had been unfortunate was clear, but the reasons for this remained unclear and the suspicions mighty indeed . . .'

p 138 House of Lords Enquiry; *Parliamentary Debates* 228–48: *H of L MSS passim*. p 139 Defoe's view; Daniel Defoe: *The History of the Union*

(Edinburgh, 1709) preface. p 139 Leven's anxieties; *H of L MSS, passim.* p 140 Kersland and the Cameronians; *The Lockhart Papers* I 302-9. p 140 Atholl and the Jacobite peers; *H of L MSS* xi p 142 Hamilton and the '08; Lockhart *Memoirs* 362-3, 381. p 144 Lord Griffin; *DNB.* p 144 The Stirlingshire gentry; *H of L MSS* and Chambers *op. cit.* III. 345 p 145 Hamilton's death; the *Lockhart Papers* I 401-10, also Marshall op. cit. 228-9. p 146 Lovat's revenge; Fergusson *op. cit.* I 93 and II 97. p 146 in a Prestonpans inn; J Kinsley (ed.) Rev. Alexander Carlyle *Anecdotes and Characters of the Times* (London 1973) 30-32. p 147 Kersland's conversation with Queensberry; Ker, *Memoirs* 44.

# *Dramatis Personae*

ABERDEEN, George Gordon, 1st Earl of (1637–1720), Jacobite sympathies.

ANNANDALE, William Johnstone, 2nd Earl and 1st Marquis of, briefly Lord Privy Seal of Scotland from 1702 but then opposed the Union; '. . . no man whatsoever placed any trust in him. Even those of the Revolution Party only employ'd him as the Indians worship the Devil, out of fear'. (Lockhart, *Memoirs* 44); d. 1721.

ANNE (1665–1714), the last Stuart sovereign, Queen of England, Scotland and Ireland from 1702, Queen of Great Britain and Ireland from 1707.

ARGYLL, Archibald Campbell, Earl of, later 1st Duke of, '. . . always an enemy to the Loyal Interst . . . altogether addicted to a lewd profligate life'. (Lockhart, *Memoirs* 44) d. 1703.

ARGYLL, John Campbell, 2nd Duke of (1678–1743), Queen's commissioner to Scotland 1705, served under Marlborough 1706–9, repressed the 'Fifteen, created Duke of Greenwich 1719; 'His head ran more upon the camp than the court . . . endowed with a cheerful and lively temper and personal valour'. (Lockhart, *Memoirs*, 133).

ATHOLL, John Murray, 2nd Marquis and 1st Duke of (1660–1724), '. . . his vanity and ambition extended so far that he could not suffer an equal'. (Lockhart, *Memoirs* 62).

BERWICK, James Fitzjames, Duke of (1670–1734), bastard of James II and VII by Arabella Churchill, Maréchal de France 1706, victor of Almanza in 1707, killed in action in Germany.

BREADALBANE, John Campbell, 1st Earl of (1635–1716), a Campbell but with strong Jacobite sympathies.

BYNG, Sir George, Viscount Torrington (1663–1733), at battle off Malaga in 1704, vice-admiral 1705, commanded squadron which saw off Forbin in 1708, his greater success the destruction of a Spanish fleet off Cape Passaro in 1718.

CADOGAN, William (1675–1726), major-general in 1706, commanded in Flanders in 1708, Marlborough's able and trusted colleague.

CARNEGY, Father ('Mr Hall'), Catholic priest and confidant of 4th Duke of Hamilton.

CHAMILLART, Michel de (1657–1721), France's Finance Minister from 1699 and also War Minister from 1701, relieved of office 1709.

CHEVREUSE, Charles Honoré d'Albert, Duc de (1646–1712), quasi-minister in Louis XIV's council.

COCHRANE, William, of Kilmaronock, Dumbartonshire laird, uncle of 4th Earl of Dundonald, Jacobite.

CUNNINGHAME, James of Aiket, major in the Scots army, sought to raise the south-west against Union, betrayed the plot, rewarded by government after the Union.

DANGEAU, Philippe de Courcillon, marquis de (1638–1720), court-watcher at Versailles.

DEFOE, Daniel (1660–1731), the celebrated author and propogandist, Harley's secret agent in Edinburgh 1706–8.

DRUMMOND, James, Lord. [Marquis of], later 2nd titular Duke of Perth, Jacobite, d. 1720, in exile.

DUNDONALD, John Cochrane, 4th Earl of, apparently had Jacobite sympathies d. 1720.

EGLINTON, Alexander Montgomerie, 9th Earl of (1660–1729), father-in-law of George Lockhart of Carnwath, Jacobite sympathies.

ERROL, Anne, Countess of, sister of 1st Duke of Perth, widowed in 1706, hostess to Hooke on his two Scottish visits, Jacobite.

ERROL, Charles Hay, 13th Earl of, Jacobite, '. . . did not make a great outward appearance at the first view yet was a man of good understanding, great honour and loyalty' (Lockhart, *Memoirs* 180), d. 1717.

FLEMING, the Hon. Charles, brother of the Earl of Wigton, Jacobite, agent between Scotland and France in 1705 and 1707–8, d. 1745.

FLETCHER, Andrew, of Saltoun (1653–1716), anti-monarchical, anti-union East Lothian laird, '. . . stuck close to the Country Party and was their Cicero'. (Lockhart *Memoirs* 71).

FORBIN, Claude, Comte de (1656–1733), French naval hero who commanded the Franco-Jacobite invasion fleet in 1708.

GEORGE, H.R.H. Prince George of Denmark (1653–1708) husband to Queen Anne, Lord High Admiral of England, 'very fat, loves News, his Bottle and the Queen' (*Memoirs of the Secret Services of John Macky*), London (Roxburghe Club) 1895, p. 33.

GLASGOW, David, 1st Earl of, supporter of the Union, 'proud, arrogant, greedy, extremely false' (Lockhart, *Memoirs* 100), d. 1733.

GODOLPHIN, Sydney, Earl (1645–1712), Lord High Treasurer under Queen Anne, dismissed 1710.

GORDON, Elizabeth Howard, Duchess of, Jacobite, English by birth, estranged wife of 1st Duke of Gordon.

HAMILTON, Anne, Duchess of in her own right (1632–1716), devout Presbyterian, mother of 4th Duke.

HAMILTON, James Douglas, 4th Duke of (1658–1712), Earl of Arran until he assumed ducal title in 1698, leader of the Scottish 'Patriots' but ambivalent Jacobite, Duke of Brandon 1711, killed in duel.

HARLEY, Robert, later 1st Earl of Oxford (1661–1724), Queen Anne's Secretary of State for the Northern Department, 1705–8; 'If any man was ever born under a necessity of being a Knave, he was.' (1st Earl Cowper, quoted in D.N.B.).

HOME, Charles Home, 6th Earl of d. 1706, Jacobite, 'one cannot imagine how great a loss the Royal Family and Country Party sustained by [his death]' (Lockhart), *Memoirs* 215.

HOME, Alexander, 7th Earl of, succeeding his father in 1707, Jacobite, d. 1720.

HOOKE, Nathaniel (1664–1738), Torcy's agent for Scottish affairs, colonel in the French army from c. 1700, brigadier from 1708, later Maréchal de camp, created Lord Hooke in the Jacobite peerage 1708, 'a man of unquestionable courage, a penetrating genius . . .' (Lovat, *op. cit.* 228) '. . . a mettle, pragmatical fellow . . . extremely vain and haughty.' (Lockhart, *Memoirs* 197f.).

JAMES, Francis Edward Stuart, Chevalier de St George (1688–1766), only son of

James II and VII and Mary of Modena, recognised by France as King of England, Scotland and Ireland 1701, attempted invasion of Scotland in 1708, briefly in Scotland at the tail end of the 'Fifteen.

JAMES II of England, VII of Scotland, (1633–1701), Duke of York until he succeeded Charles II in 1685, fled to France 1688 but still considered himself to be King.

KER, John, of Kersland, government spy 1706–7, memoirs published 1726, d. in King's bench prison that year.

KILSYTH, William Livingstone, 3rd Viscount, Jacobite, 'out' in the 'Fifteen, d. in exile 1733.

KINNARD, Patrick Kinnard, 3rd Baron, Jacobite, d. 1715.

LINLITHGOW, James Livingston, 5th Earl of, Jacobite, 'out' in the 'Fifteen, d. in exile, 1723.

LEVEN, David Melville, 3rd Earl of and 2nd Earl of Melville (1660–1728); 'He was born and bred an enemy to the Royal Family . . . however he was no ways severe'. (Lockhart, *Memoirs*, 99).

LOCKHART, George, of Carnwath (1673–1731), Jacobite, lifelong friend of 4th Duke of Hamilton, wrote the *Memoirs* after 1707, imprisoned in the 'Fifteen, confidential agent of the Old Pretender in Scotland, 1718–27, died in a duel.

LOUDEN, Hugh, Earl of Louden, '. . . though he pursued his own aims and designs, yet it was in a moderate, gentlemany way'. (Lockhart, *Memoirs* 99).

LOUIS XIV (1638–1715), King of France from 1643.

LOVAT, Simon Fraser, 11th Baron (1667–1747), outlawed for outrage on the Dowager Lady Lovat 1701, professed Jacobitism and was principal in the 'Scots Plot' 1703, in custody in France 1704–15, raised his clan for King George in the 'Fifteen but Jacobite again in the 'Forty-five, beheaded in 1747.

MACKAY, Major-General Hugh of Scourie, served in the Scots Brigade in the service of Holland, commanded the Scottish army at Killiecrankie 1689, killed at battle of Steinkirk 1694.

MACLEAN, Sir John, 4th Bart, at Killiecrankie, 'peached' on his fellow Jacobite conspirators in 1703, brought out his clan in the 'Fifteen.

MAINTENON, Mme de (1635–1719), wife of Louis XIV but not queen, friend of Mary of Modena and thus a pro-Jacobite influence.

MAR, John Erskine, 6th Earl of (1675–1732), supporter of Union, Secretary of State for Scotland in 1709 but led the 'Fifteen (disastrously), died in exile, '. . . a man of good sense but bad morals' (Lockhart *Memoirs*, 139).

MARISCHAL, Mary, Countess, Daughter of 1st Duke of Perth, Jacobite.

MARISCHAL, William Keith, 9th Earl, Jacobite, d. 1712 '. . . too bent on his pleasures'. (Lockhart, *Memoirs* 181).

MARLBOROUGH, John Churchill, 1st Duke of (1650–1722), Queen Anne's Captain-General, 'of a wonderful presence of mind, so as hardly ever to be discomposed; of a very clear head and sound judgement' (Macky, op cit 35).

MARY of Modena (1658–1718), James' second queen and mother of the Old Pretender.

MATIGNON, Charles Auguste de, Comte de Gacé, Maréchal de France (1647–1729), commander of land forces for the invasion of Scotland in 1708.

MIDDLETON, Charles Middleton, 2nd Earl of (1640–1719), secretary of state at the court of St Germain.

MORAY, Charles Stewart, 6th Earl of, Jacobite, d. 1715.

MORAY, Captain John, later Lieutenant-Colonel, brother to the Laird of Abercairney in Strathearn, officer in the French service, died of wounds 1710.

NAIRNE, William Murray, 2nd Baron, brother of 2nd Duke of Atholl, Jacobite.

NICHOLSON, Thomas Joseph, Catholic and Jacobite, first Vicar-General in Scotland 1695, d. 1718.

NITHSDALE, William Maxwell, 5th Earl of (1676–1744), Jacobite, 'out' in the 'Fifteen, died in exile.

OGILVIE, James, younger of Boyne, Jacobite, Brigadier in the Jacobite army in the 'Fifteen, died in exile c. 1728.

PANMURE, James Maule, 4th Earl of (1659–1723), Jacobite, 'out' in the 'Fifteen, died in exile.

PERTH, James Drummond, 5th Earl and 1st titular Duke of (1648–1716), Chancellor at St Germain, accompanied James in the attempt on Scotland in 1708.

PONTCHARTRAIN, Jérome Phélypeaux, comte de, (1674–1747); Louis XIV's minister for the navy from 1699.

QUEENSBERRY, James Douglas, 2nd Duke of (1662–1711), architect of Union, created Duke of Dover 1707; 'To outward appearance and in his ordinary conversation, he was of a gentle and good disposition, inwardly a very Devil standing at nothing to advance his own Interest and Designs'. (Lockhart, *Memoirs* 9).

SAINT-SIMON, Louis de Rouvroy, Duc de (1675–1755), author of the famous *Mémoires*.

SEAFIELD, James Ogilvy, 4th Earl of Findlater and 1st Earl of Seafield, (1664–1730).

STAIR, John Dalrymple, 1st Earl of (1648–1707), '. . . author of the barbarous murder of Glencoe . . . 'Twas he that was at the bottom of the Union.' (Lockhart, *Memoirs*, 95).

STORMONT, David Murray, 5th Viscount, Jacobite, (fortunately) imprisoned during the 'Fifteen, d. 1731.

STRATHMORE, John Lyon, 4th Earl of, Jacobite, d. 1712.

THOMPSON, Sir John, 1st Baron Haversham (1647–1710), vociferous opponent of Queen Anne's ministers.

TORCY, Colbert, Jean-Baptiste, Marquis de (1665–1746), Secretary of State to Louis XIV.

WILLIAM, Prince of Orange (1650–1702) William III of England from 1688, King of Scotland from 1689 (in joint monarchy with his wife Mary, daughter of James II until her death in 1694).

# Index